Cambridge English

Level 6

Series editor: Philip Prowse

This Time
It's Personal

Alan Battersby

CAMBRIDGE
UNIVERSITY PRESS

PUBLISHED BY THE PRESS SYNDICATE OF THE UNIVERSITY OF CAMBRIDGE
The Pitt Building, Trumpington Street, Cambridge, United Kingdom

CAMBRIDGE UNIVERSITY PRESS
The Edinburgh Building, Cambridge CB2 2RU, UK
40 West 20th Street, New York, NY 10011-4211, USA
477 Williamstown Road, Port Melbourne, VIC 3207, Australia
Ruiz de Alarcón 13, 28014 Madrid, Spain
Dock House, The Waterfront, Cape Town 8001, South Africa

http://www.cambridge.org

First published 2003
Reprinted 2004

Printed in the United Kingdom at the University Press, Cambridge

Front cover photograph by Emma Louise Morris

Typeface 12/15pt Adobe Garamond   *System* 3B2 [CE]

ISBN 0 521 79844 2 (paperback)
ISBN 0 521 79845 0 (cassette)

Contents

Characters

Nat Marley: New York private investigator
Stella Delgado: Nat Marley's personal assistant
Captain Oldenberg: detective with the New York Police
    Department (NYPD)
Joe Blaney: colleague of Nat Marley, ex-NYPD
José De La Cruz: Stella's brother
Lena Rosenthal: Nat Marley's lawyer
Mrs. Romanov: Russian widow
Victor Kamenev: Russian businessman
Edith Tilden (Edie): old lady
Commander Jim Lockhart: commander of the Coast
    Guard Group, Moriches
Miguel and Carlos: friends of José De la Cruz
Ed Winchester: journalist on the *Daily News*
Mossolov: professional criminal
Zernov: works for Mossolov
Tchernov: Russian immigrant

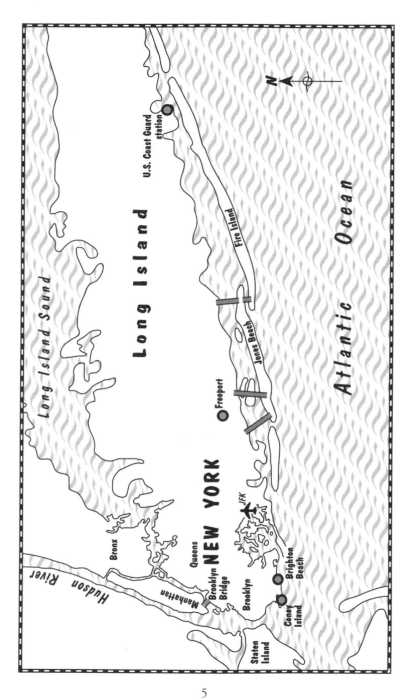

Long Island Sound

Long Island

U.S. Coast Guard station

Fire Island

Jones Beach

Freeport

Atlantic Ocean

Hudson River

Bronx

Queens

NEW YORK

Manhattan

Brooklyn Bridge

Brooklyn

Staten Island

Coney Island

Brighton Beach

JFK

N

5

Chapter 1 *New York in the spring*

It was a fine but chilly spring morning. Fine enough even to make the New York borough of Queens seem attractive. Like any other day, I left my apartment on Main Street, Queens, and walked to the subway station to commute into midtown Manhattan on the number seven train. Like any other day, I read the *New York Daily News* to pass the time during the journey. Out of professional interest, I always glance through the day's fresh crime stories. Muggings, thefts, a car-jacking, a shooting, a bank robbery, and so on. Crime – the unpleasant reality of life from which I make my living.

The name's Marley, Nat Marley, licensed private investigator. My prediction is that you already have a mental image of my type of work. I can safely bet that that your image comes straight from the fantasy world of Hollywood. That's a long way from the truth. The majority of my work is dull. Often just pure routine stuff like divorce, bad debts, or missing persons. Don't imagine for a moment that I'm good-looking either. Just an ordinary-looking guy, bald, overweight and on the wrong side of forty. And let's get another thing straight, my working days seldom start with a wealthy, attractive female client anxiously waiting for my professional services.

My office is on East 43rd Street, just a couple of blocks from Grand Central Station. Stella Delgado, my personal assistant was already at her desk talking on the phone.

Stella's been with me most of the time I've been in business. A beautiful, intelligent Puerto Rican in her late twenties. If she wanted, she could get a far better job elsewhere. And I've told her that too. But she insists on working for me; she must like me. You've heard of the expression 'on the wrong side of the tracks', meaning the poor, underprivileged areas of the inner city? That's where Stella grew up, in the Barrio on the Upper East Side, known as Spanish Harlem. She had left school early and got into plenty of trouble as a kid. Then it took years of night school study to catch up on her education.

As she put down the phone, I asked, "How are things on this beautiful spring morning?"

Silence. She just gave me a blank stare. The morning mail was on her desk, unopened. Something was definitely wrong. "Stella, what's the matter? Come on, out with it."

She looked up at me tearfully. "Nat, I don't know what to do. It's family – my kid brother, José. I've just been talking to him on the phone. He's been arrested. He could be in serious trouble."

There was work to catch up with that morning, bills to send out to our satisfied or dissatisfied clients, and some annoying letters from the IRS, the tax people. Yet again, they'd claimed I hadn't paid enough tax. But clients and the IRS would have to wait.

"Stella, tell me everything."

"It's a long story. José was found by the police in the early hours of this morning on 112th Street just off Lexington Avenue, Upper East Side. He was lying unconscious with head injuries, in the driver's seat of a car that had crashed into a wall in a parking lot. Nat, he doesn't even own a car. Anyway, he was taken to the emergency room at Metropolitan Hospital. Now he's in a secure room under police guard. He was allowed to make one phone call, so he called me."

"So what's the story? How did he get into this mess?" I asked.

"The awful thing is he has no memory of what he was doing," Stella said. "All he can remember is being at some bar in Brighton Beach with his buddies yesterday evening. Then nothing."

"Has he been charged with anything?" I asked.

"No. At least, not as far as I know," replied Stella.

"Why were José and his buddies going out for a drink at Brighton Beach, anyway? That's quite a way from Spanish Harlem for a night out."

"José works in the summer at a diner on Surf Avenue, Coney Island. The place closes up in the winter. José had been to see his boss to confirm his job for next summer. He got some good news – they took him on as a cook. José had taken a couple of his buddies along to see if he could fix up work for them. They were taken on as waiters. Good money, plus room and board, starting first of April. Afterwards, they went out to celebrate."

The thought of Coney Island brought back some of those golden childhood memories: trips to Coney Island beach and the rides at the amusement park, family vacations at the beach. I put those thoughts to the back of my mind and concentrated on Stella's story.

"Anything more?" I asked.

"He said he had just a vague memory of a bar somewhere on Brighton Beach Avenue. He knew he'd had a few too many drinks. Then nothing until he woke up in a hospital bed."

"Maybe he's in shock," I suggested. "Temporary memory loss. If this was a simple case of drunk-driving, he wouldn't be under police guard. And where did he get the car from?"

"I don't know, Nat. José's never had a driver's license."

Not having a driver's license didn't mean he hadn't stolen the car and driven it anyway. But I didn't say that to Stella.

I thought for a moment. If José hadn't been charged with any offense, the NYPD could only hold him for a limited time.

"All right, Stella. This is what we'll do. If José hasn't been formally charged, there's no reason why we shouldn't be allowed to visit. We're going straight over to the hospital to talk with him."

Stella didn't move but just stood by her desk, biting her lip.

"Is something else bothering you?" I asked.

"Nat, I'm worried sick. José's an ordinary loveable guy who likes a good time. OK, he's got a criminal record. He got into some trouble when he was a teenager. But I know he's harmless. A danger to nobody. But someone with his background . . . you know as well as I do what conclusion the police will come to."

"Come on, Stella," I said. "Things have changed in this city. It's not like the bad old days. You know how sensitive the police are nowadays about any question of possible prejudice. You can't assume that the NYPD will think José is guilty because of his background. Any suspect has to be judged on the evidence."

"Maybe you're right," she replied, simply.

Stella didn't seem to be convinced. But I knew the NYPD would go to any lengths to avoid the kind of publicity an accusation of racial prejudice would attract. I also understood Stella's fears. Stella and her family are Puerto Rican. During the 1950s tens of thousands of Puerto Ricans emigrated from their island to the U.S.A. When they arrived, some of them discovered that the U.S.A. wasn't the land of opportunity they'd expected. Some had exchanged the poverty of Puerto Rico for the poor neighborhoods of New York. There were dead-end jobs waiting for them as kitchen hands or unskilled factory workers. Today, however, some have succeeded in creating a good life – like Stella, with a permanent job, comfortable apartment, and loving husband. But for Stella it had been a struggle. I could appreciate how her culture and background might affect the way she saw things.

"Lock up the office and let's go," I said.

Chapter 2 *Metropolitan Hospital*

After a few inquiries at the main reception desk, we were finally given the location of José's room at the hospital. Eventually, when we reached the floor, it was obvious that gaining access would be no simple matter. There was a bored-looking police officer sitting outside. I thought I might start with a little gentle persuasion. It can sometimes work, even on police officers. I should know – I used to be an NYPD officer before I set up my own business.

"Excuse me," I said, showing the officer my investigator's license. "I represent Mr. José De La Cruz. Would it be possible to speak to him? The lady here is Ms. Delgado, sister of Mr. De La Cruz."

The officer was unimpressed. He looked me up and down and said flatly, "Sorry, sir. No one's allowed in. And that's official."

I wondered if he was going to be one of those people who get their job satisfaction by creating difficulties for others. I wasn't going to take 'no' as the final answer. "Come on, now. Just a quick word. Won't do any harm."

"No," replied the officer sharply. "This guy's a suspect. He's wanted for questioning."

"Suspected of doing what?" I demanded. "Has he been charged with any crime?"

"Don't know, and no."

"Thanks for all your co-operation. Give me the name of your boss, will you?" I asked.

It was Captain Oldenberg. A familiar name. Oldenberg and I had worked together at the NYPD. That was over fifteen years ago, when we'd both been patrolmen on the streets of the Lower East Side. Since I'd left the NYPD to become a private eye, Oldenberg had risen through the ranks and had now been promoted to captain. Every now and then our professional paths crossed. Oldenberg was the sort of guy you didn't forget in a hurry. He could be bad-tempered, loud, and dominating at times. Despite that, he was basically a good cop. I'd need all my charm to deal with him, though.

"Thanks. I'll be back," I said.

Stella was looking furious. "Nat! Exactly what is going on here?" she demanded as we walked away from the room. "Are you just going to take 'no' for an answer?"

"Stay calm, Stella. In this situation we need friends, not enemies. I'll call Oldenberg."

I phoned police headquarters and was put through to Oldenberg's office. He wasn't exactly pleased to hear from me. That was normal. He was even less pleased when I asked if José was free to leave once the doctors had given him the all clear.

"You've got to be joking, Marley!" he shouted. "There's no way I'm going to let that guy out on the streets. He's being held on 'reasonable suspicion'. I've had a crime scene team examining the car De La Cruz was found in, and I'm waiting for the results of forensic tests."

Tests to examine what? Bloodstains on clothes? DNA? A weapon? I tried my charm on Oldenberg again.

"I'd be interested to know what those tests would be for," I said.

"Sure you would. Marley, you know I can't reveal any details of evidence until the suspect has been charged."

It was the answer I'd been expecting. No harm in having another try.

"Have you established who was the owner of the vehicle?" I asked hopefully.

"Same as my previous answer," he replied bluntly.

I got the impression that the captain was enjoying himself. One last attempt to make some progress.

"OK, Oldenberg. I know your position. Rules have to be obeyed. But if my client hasn't been charged, why can't I speak to him? I have his sister with me and she's upset in a big way. Just ten minutes? And I'll agree to the police officer being present too."

"All right, Marley. Have your ten minutes. I'll call the officer and tell him to expect you."

We hurried back to speak to José. The officer showed us into his room. José was sitting up in bed, with a bandage around his head and an IV drip attached to his arm. There was a hopeless expression on his face. Stella went over to him, took his hand, and spoke to him gently.

"How are you feeling, José?"

"Not great. I'm full of painkillers, but I can still feel my head spinning," said José. "Stella, it's real good to see you. Are you going to get me out of here? I haven't done anything wrong."

"You and I both know you haven't done anything wrong," she said. "Remember what I told you, José. You've got to keep holding on."

"So what's the cop doing here, huh?" asked José, glancing in the direction of the officer.

"We had to agree to the officer being present. José, this is my boss, Nat Marley. He's going to help you."

"I'm sure glad to see you, Nat," said José.

"If we're going to help you, you've got to give us the whole story. Don't hold anything back." I said. "Everything that happened from the time you left home yesterday until you woke up in this hospital bed."

José, with his two friends, Miguel and Carlos, took the subway to Coney Island to find work. The boss at the diner offered him a job as a cook and José's buddies were taken on as waiters. José showed Miguel and Carlos around the sights of Coney Island during the afternoon. After stopping for food, they moved on to Brighton Beach to celebrate. By early evening they'd had several drinks in bars on Brighton Beach Avenue, in the heart of the Russian community. He had a confused memory of waking up in a bar. His buddies had gone. Then nothing. The next thing he remembered was waking up in Metropolitan Hospital.

"You don't remember anything else?" I asked.

"Nothing. It's the honest truth, Nat," said José. "It's all a black fog."

"Brighton Beach? Kind of an unusual night out for three guys from Upper Manhattan, huh?" I asked.

"You're right. At first it felt kind of strange for us to be there," said José, "but people were nice and didn't mind three outsiders having a night out. One bartender got friendly when we asked him about all the different vodkas."

"Now think hard, José. Can you remember anything else?" I asked.

"Nothing," he replied.

"What happened to Miguel and Carlos?"

"I can't remember."

It didn't look good. José had been found unconscious at the wheel of a car that wasn't his. He had no memory of what had happened after passing out in a Brighton Beach bar.

"José, I know you don't have a driver's license, but can you drive?" I asked.

"No way, Nat. I've never tried. And even if I could, I'd have been too drunk to drive."

The police officer interrupted us: "Time's up, Mr. Marley."

There wasn't any point in asking for more time. I didn't think we were going to learn anything more of value. As to what had actually happened, it was still a complete mystery. Was José the victim or was he the guilty party? My impression of him from our brief talk was of a harmless ordinary guy; a guy who had gotten into some sort of trouble and had no explanation for what had happened.

It wasn't looking good. There was some small hope though, since I'd gotten clients out of worse situations than this. José needed a lawyer, urgently, and I knew just the woman for the job: Lena Rosenthal. She was capable, intelligent, and tough; someone who could stand up to Oldenberg. As soon as José was charged with a crime, then we would have something concrete from the NYPD. Otherwise, we were just operating in the dark.

Stella had to get back to her family, so I gave her the rest of the day off. I just wished I could say something that might give her some comfort. But I knew whatever I said would be inadequate. Once I had more information, then I might be able to offer her some hope.

The next day, the temperature was close to freezing. A layer of frost covered the windows of cars parked on the street overnight. I'd arrived at the office early and was just putting the breakfast coffee and donuts down on the desk when the phone rang. A familiar voice barked at me – Captain Oldenberg.

"Marley? Just calling to tell you that your client De La Cruz is still being held at the hospital. I wanted to get him moved to headquarters for further questioning, but the doctors insisted he be kept under observation. I'm still waiting for the results of the tests on bloodstains found on his jacket and a wallet in his possession."

Oldenberg had given away a few more details. Bloodstains? Things were getting more serious.

In desperation I said: "Oldenberg, my client can't drive. And what's more, the alcohol level from the blood tests should indicate he'd have been incapable of driving anyway."

"Marley, don't make me laugh," he replied.

"My client needs to consult his lawyer. With your permission, I'd like to take her over to the hospital this morning. Any objections?"

"Be my guest, Marley. I'll call the officer on duty and tell him to expect you."

By now Stella had arrived. I told her the latest developments. She took it all in silently then sat in front of her computer with her head in her hands. I arranged to pick up Lena Rosenthal.

Later, as our cab headed up First Avenue towards the hospital, I gave Lena all the details she needed about José's case. I also explained how I was involved.

"Lena, this isn't just a routine case for me. This guy's the kid brother of my assistant, Stella Delgado. Stella's been working for me so long that she's like part of my family. I feel responsible for both Stella and José. You could say it's personal this time."

Lena nodded. "Thanks for telling me, Nat. Anything else I should know?"

"I should warn you about Captain Oldenberg. He has a reputation for being aggressive and insensitive."

"Oldenberg and I have met before. I know what to expect," replied Lena.

At the hospital, before we saw José, a doctor took us aside.

"Excuse me. Are you family?" she asked.

"We represent Mr. De La Cruz. The name's Nat Marley, private investigator," I replied, flashing my I.D. at the doctor. "This is his lawyer Ms. Rosenthal. We have permission from the NYPD to visit our client."

"Thank you. I'm Dr. Ericson. Mr. De La Cruz has been under my care since he was admitted. His condition has been giving me cause for concern. In the accident, he received a heavy blow to the head. So far his condition has been stable, but there have been some symptoms that worry me. He's complained about seeing double images and he has twice lost consciousness, though very briefly. And also there's some memory loss. So, I must warn you not to put Mr. De La Cruz under any unnecessary stress. He's been through enough already, and with any further stress . . ."

"Understood, Doctor. We'll take great care."

Before seeing José, Lena turned to me. "It would be a

good idea not to mention anything about the forensic tests. This guy sounds scared enough already."

I nodded my agreement.

Eventually we were allowed in to speak to José. He looked at us with dull eyes and raised a hand to acknowledge us. I could see the despair in his eyes. Lena went over exactly the same questions as I had asked before. There was nothing more that José could add. We had made no further progress. As we were leaving, José cried out hopelessly: "Nat, for God's sake, get me out of here! I'm going out of my mind."

Chapter 3 *Jones Beach*

Saturday morning was cold but bright. I was feeling fit and active. I started the day by following my Saturday routine. Buying the *Daily News* and wandering down Main Street, Queens, to Slim Pete's Diner. Breakfast there was always reliable – unhealthy but very tasty. Maybe that explained 'Slim' Pete's weight problem.

"Morning, Nat," said Slim Pete. "Why so cheerful?"

"Pete, I now realize that a healthy lifestyle is no solution to a mid-life crisis – which means I'll have one of your breakfast specials and plenty of coffee."

As I worked my way through breakfast, I looked through the *Daily News*. There was a story about a murder victim. A guy by the name of Alexei Romanov. Where had I heard the name 'Romanov' before? That was it, the old Russian royal family. The body had been found late Friday afternoon, floating in Coney Island Creek. The victim had been shot in the head and had been dead for over twenty-four hours. There were some more details. Romanov owned some kind of business on Brighton Beach. He was involved in a society that helped immigrants from Russia to settle and adapt to life in the U.S.A. His tearful widow told reporters that she had no idea who could have done such a thing. He seemed to have been a well-liked and respected man who was active in the community. I hoped and prayed there was no connection with José.

Another story caught my eye. The headline read: 'Wreck

on Jones Beach'. Part of a lifeboat had been washed up on the shore. Two bodies had been found nearby. No further details. I'd been brought up on Staten Island. As a kid, just taking the ferry across to Manhattan seemed like a big adventure. A day out on Coney Island was a real trip, but Jones Beach, on Long Island, felt like going abroad. Maybe there's something of that kid still left inside me. I still get a thrill when I get way out of the city and stand on the beach looking out at the Atlantic, watching the waves crashing. Why not escape from the city for the day? The ocean air would do me good.

I was folding up the newspaper when Slim Pete came over to chat.

"So what's New York's smartest private eye doing? Putting more gangsters behind bars?" he asked.

"Funny you should say that," I answered. "New York's criminal community can relax. I've just decided I'm going to spend a day at the beach."

"Huh! A life of leisure. It's all right for some people."

I took the bus from Main Street, to Jamaica Station. You can connect there with the Long Island Rail Road to Freeport. From there, I took a cab to Jones Beach, a long narrow strip of land about two miles from the mainland. There was a real chill in the wind coming in off the ocean. Enough to keep any crowds away so early in the year. In the height of the season, thousands of New Yorkers crowd into the area to claim their little piece of beach. But today I could walk without tripping over beach towels or bumping into umbrellas.

I strolled along the shore for about an hour, then returned. Unusually energetic for me, but I felt better afterwards. The air was clean and fresh. Then I stood for a while on the Atlantic side, watching the waves crash onto the beach. I knew why I had really come here. It was the reports of the bodies washed up on the beach. It was my day off, but I was still playing the investigator. That was why my marriage had broken up. My wife never saw much of me when I was with the NYPD. When I started out on my own as a private investigator she saw even less of me. Then one day she walked out on me. She left a note which said that I just didn't give her enough attention and she couldn't carry on like that. The sad truth was she was right. If there's ever a second Mrs. Marley, she'll have to be one very tolerant lady to put up with me.

I wandered over to a group of bars and restaurants which would be packed with visitors in a few weeks. One or two were already open, while in others work was going on in preparation for the coming season. Outside a bar an old guy up on a ladder was painting. He looked down at me from his work.

"You're out of luck if you want a drink, mister. We don't open till the first of April," he said.

"Just wanted to talk if it's not holding you up," I replied.

"Go ahead and talk, mister. I'm just doing this as a favor for my son-in-law. He doesn't care how slowly I work."

"I see Jones Beach has been in the news. Some story about a lifeboat found wrecked along the shore and two bodies," I said.

The old man came down from the ladder. A good sign. I had got his interest. He pointed west along the shore with a dripping paintbrush.

21

"The wrecked lifeboat was found about a mile west along the beach. There's an old lady – when I say old, she's a good ten years older than me. Well, she goes beachcombing regularly. You know, looking for shells and stuff. She found the wreck and the bodies."

"Really! Must have been quite a shock for her," I said.

"I don't know about that, mister. It made her day. Never seen her so excited."

It was time to make my move. I showed him my investigator's license.

"Gee! A real private eye!" exclaimed the old man. "I would've expected someone . . ."

"Someone younger and better-looking?" I interrupted. "We come in all shapes and sizes. Look, I'm investigating this wreck for a client," I lied. "I'd like to talk to this lady. Who is she, and where can I find her?"

"Her name's Edith Tilden. People call her 'Edie'. She's English, but she's lived here for years. She looks kind of eccentric, but she's OK once you get talking. See that place over there?"

The old man pointed toward a beat-up building with the sign 'Ornella's Italian Clam House' above the entrance.

"She'll probably be in there," he continued. "She claims Ornella's the only person on Jones Beach who can make a good cup of tea."

Life's full of surprises. Since when did Italians make good tea? I entered the restaurant. It didn't look open for business. Most of the tables and chairs were piled up in a corner. Only a handful of tables were set. At one of the tables sat a little old lady dressed in bright yellow and purple. A plump, cheerful woman welcomed me.

"Morning, mister. No hot food until April. Just snacks and hot and cold drinks." she said.

"I was looking for a sandwich and a cup of tea. I've been told that you make the best tea in Jones Beach," I replied.

The old woman at the table looked up and said, "You've come to the right place for tea."

"Then make that two teas – one for the lady here."

I went over to her table. "Mind if I join you?" I asked.

"Not at all," she answered. "Take a seat."

I noticed the way she spoke. Not the slightest American accent.

"Thanks. You English?" I asked.

"I'm probably as American as you are, now. I've been in the U.S.A. for fifty years but never lost the accent or the tea-drinking habit. The name's Edie, Edie Tilden."

"Pleased to meet you. I'm Nat Marley."

The sandwich and teas were brought over to the table. After small talk about the weather, it was time to get some information. I showed Edie my private investigator's license. Her eyes grew large and round and her mouth dropped open. This old lady was deeply impressed. I wish I had that effect on people more often.

"I hear you found the wrecked lifeboat and two bodies on the beach. I'm investigating the wreck for a client," I lied again.

Edie waved her teaspoon at me excitedly. "Mr. Marley, I've been walking up and down this beach for years. I've found bits and pieces of boats, but never a body. Two real dead bodies! What do you say to that?" she asked.

"Must have been a terrible shock," I said.

"People don't look pretty after they've been in the sea."

"Can you describe them?" I asked.

"Certainly. Two young men, could be anywhere in their twenties. Medium height. Thin. Both of them looked as if they needed a good meal. Short hair. They hadn't shaved for days. Cheap-looking clothes. One of them had a gold cross on a chain around his neck. I've never seen one like it before. Let me show you."

She paused, took a clean paper napkin from the table, found a pencil in her pocket, and drew a picture of a cross with two horizontal bars, the top one a little shorter. Then at the base of the cross, a short bar at a forty-five degree angle. I didn't recognize it.

"Thanks. Mind if I keep this?" I asked. "Now what can you remember about the boat?"

"What I found was the rear half. Probably from a boat big enough to fit a dozen people in. It had seen better days, though."

"What do you mean?"

"The wood was rotten with age. Some of it was so soft I could break off pieces with my bare hands. It looked like someone had been trying to repair it, but hadn't made a good job of it. The boat must have split in two."

"Were there any identifying marks? Like names or numbers?" I asked.

"Some letters at the back, maybe the boat's name," Edie answered. "I couldn't make out a complete word, but it looked like a foreign language. And that's about all I can tell you. The Coast Guard took it away so there's nothing to see now."

"Thanks. You've been very helpful. Here's my card. Where can I contact you if I need to speak to you again?"

She wrote a Freeport address and phone number on the paper. I left Edie and did some more beach walking. I felt relaxed and content when I finally got back to Queens that evening. But there was still the problem of José. Unless I turned up some new evidence soon, he could be facing a long prison sentence.

The next day I woke up early but was feeling active. It must have been the effect of all that exercise the day before. There are various ways to spend your Sunday. Unfortunately, I had to go into the office to sort out some accounts. On the subway, I glanced through the Sunday edition of the *Daily News*. It didn't have anything to add to yesterday's stories. At the office on East 43rd Street, I was trying to make sense of the previous year's accounts when the phone rang. Who on earth wanted to speak to me at this time on a Sunday? I grabbed the phone. It was Oldenberg.

"Marley, trust you to be in the office on a Sunday. Just wanted to bring you up to date on your client."

I immediately felt tense. "Go on," I said.

"I'm on my way back from Metropolitan Hospital," said Oldenberg. "De La Cruz has been charged with murder."

Chapter 4   *East Harlem*

"Oldenberg," I began, "you've got a confused guy in a hospital bed with serious head injuries, and you add to the misery with a murder charge!"

"Just doing my job, Marley," he replied. "Following procedure."

"Who's the murder victim?" I asked.

"A guy by the name of Alexei Romanov, some businessman from Brighton Beach."

The same guy I'd read about in the *Daily News*. "OK, Oldenberg. You'd better explain how you reached the conclusion that my client's a killer."

Oldenberg went on to give me the details. The cause of death was a shot to the head from the pistol which was found in the car. José's fingerprints were on the handle and trigger. The results of the forensic tests proved that he was the attacker. Romanov's blood was found on José's jacket. Also, the NYPD had positive identification of a wallet found in his possession – it belonged to Romanov. The police had the murder weapon, the killer, and forensic evidence. As far as Oldenberg was concerned, the investigation was closed. I had serious doubts. All the evidence pointed toward José, but what was the motive?

"OK, Oldenberg. Have you established a motive?" I asked.

"Maybe he saw the opportunity to get some easy money – a carjacking, I guess," he answered.

Again, I wasn't convinced. Could a sleepy drunk possibly be capable of carjacking and murder? "What do you mean, 'I guess'? Where's the supporting evidence? Do you have witnesses?" I asked.

"Who needs witnesses with the amount of evidence piled up against him?" Oldenberg asked.

No point in continuing the conversation. I'd learned enough. The significant point was the lack of witnesses. Oldenberg obviously thought that the forensic evidence was enough to prove José was guilty. Someone must have seen José and his buddies celebrating that night. I'd have to go to Brighton Beach to do some of my own investigating.

Meanwhile, I needed to check on José. A call to the hospital confirmed that his condition was stable, but the doctors were still keeping him under observation. It seemed unlikely that he would be allowed to leave the hospital. But José was better off there than in a cell. Another call, this time to Stella. I brought her up to date on developments. I also needed to get a clearer picture of exactly what had happened on Wednesday night. I had to speak to one of José's buddies. Stella promised to set up a meeting with them as soon as possible.

A few minutes later, Stella called back.

"Nat? I've set up a meeting with Carlos and Miguel. Can you get over here now? . . . Yes? . . . Good. We'll be at my mom's apartment, 1295 First Ave, apartment 104, on the tenth floor. That's the East River Housing, on First Avenue between 102nd and 105th Streets. We'll be expecting you. Call me on my cell phone if you have any problem finding it."

There wouldn't be any problem. The area was Spanish

Harlem, and I'd walked most of those streets when I was an NYPD patrolman. My only hope was that his buddies would remember something that had slipped José's mind, anything. I took an uptown local train from Grand Central to 103rd Street, then walked the three blocks across town to the East River Housing project. In the space of those seven subway stops, the city changes completely. In Spanish Harlem, there's not a skyscraper in sight. Only a few remaining traditional brownstone houses among the anonymous gray concrete blocks of the housing projects.

I was shown into a comfortably furnished room overlooking the East River, with a view of Wards Island at the southern tip of the Bronx. José's buddies were there. Two ordinary-looking guys in their early twenties.

Stella introduced us. "Nat. I'd like you to meet Miguel and Carlos. This is my boss, Nat. He's like family to me, and we're doing everything we can to help José. I want you to tell everything to Nat just like you told it to me."

"All of it? Again?" asked Carlos.

"Yes, every bit. You might recall something that could help José," she said.

Carlos began. Much of what they said confirmed what we already knew from José's story: the interview at the diner, the sightseeing tour of Coney Island, the bars on Brighton Beach Avenue. What I was really interested in was the final bar where José had fallen asleep.

"We ended up in this bar that had every kind of vodka you could imagine," continued Carlos. "The bartender in there got friendly when we took an interest in the drinks. He was recommending what to try."

"The name of the bar?" I asked.

"Sorry, Nat. I don't remember," replied Carlos.

"So, some bar, somewhere in Brighton Beach, selling lots of different vodkas. Could be one of many in New York's Little Odessa. Can you remember anything else about the bar?"

"The walls were covered with baseball stuff. Team photos, shirts, bats . . . that sort of thing. I remember asking the bartender, 'Hey, what's all this? Baseball in the middle of the Russian community?' Apparently the owner's a huge baseball fan."

"Good," I said. "There can't be too many bars like that in Little Odessa. How long did you stay?"

"We tried all these different flavored vodkas. After an hour or so, I knew I'd had too much. My head was spinning. José had fallen asleep, and I knew we'd have to help him home. We needed to get sober for the subway ride, so Miguel and I went out to find some black coffee. We found a place that had coffee to go. Carlos waited outside the bar with the coffees while I went inside to get José. But there was no sign of him. I asked the bartender, but he didn't know. We just thought he'd woken up and gone home."

"Thanks. You've been a great help. Call Stella if you remember anything more," I said.

Progress at last. I now had a starting point for my investigation. I had to find the bar that José and his friends had gone to. Now I had a lead: the baseball connection. Suddenly, my cell phone rang. It was Captain Oldenberg.

"Marley? It's your client De La Cruz. The guy's gone crazy. He broke out of an operating room and somehow climbed up on the roof of the hospital. He's threatening to throw himself off. He might listen to you. Can you come right now and help talk some sense into him?"

Chapter 5 *A matter of life or death*

Metropolitan Hospital is only three blocks downtown on First Avenue. Stella ran on ahead and I hurried after her. I was completely out of breath when I arrived. Outside the main entrance was a collection of various NYPD vehicles and a Fire Department truck with a ladder. Barriers had been set up around the base of the building with signs that read: 'Police line. Do not cross.' High up on the top of the building, sitting on the edge of the roof, I could make out a figure. It was José. If he jumped, there was no way he'd survive.

Among the police vehicles was a large blue van marked 'Tactical Response Unit.' That's police language, which translated means 'a negotiation team.' These are the people whose weapons are words, not guns. They will negotiate for hours or days to prevent a crime or a tragedy. I was relieved to see them here. Those guys are so calm compared to officers like Oldenberg. They wouldn't get impatient watching paint dry. If it takes forty-eight hours to prevent a potential death by talking to the guy, hour after hour, they'll do it. Persuasion, not force, is their philosophy.

Oldenberg was waiting for us outside the entrance. "Er, Marley," he began, "this is kind of embarrassing . . ."

I cut him off. "Embarrassing? It's a disaster! How on earth did my client end up on the roof?" I demanded. "I thought you had him under twenty-four-hour guard.

What's been going on here? Is this another example of NYPD inefficiency?"

As we hurried through the hospital corridors, Oldenberg raised his hands in apology. "I can't offer any excuses. Your client had been taken to an operating room. The police officer was told that De La Cruz was unconscious, so he decided to take an unofficial break outside. The medical team had to leave De La Cruz temporarily while they attended to a more urgent case. During that time, he must have regained consciousness, panicked and gone up to the roof."

An elevator took us up to the top floor. We were taken through a door marked: 'No entry.' At the foot of the stairs to the roof, Dr. Ericson was waiting. She looked nervous and anxious.

"Mr. Marley and Ms. Delgado, thank God you're here. My patient needs people he knows and trusts. You know he should be in the operating room? He was being prepared for surgery before escaping wearing only a surgical gown. He's seriously ill. I'm not trying to be dramatic, but this is a matter of life or death."

"Thanks, Doctor. I understand your concern," I said.

"One more thing, Mr. Marley. There are some curious bruise marks on Mr. De La Cruz's neck. Like someone had gripped him violently. He couldn't have received injuries like that in a car crash."

The doctor put her fingers and thumb around her throat to demonstrate.

"I told Captain Oldenberg, but he didn't seem to take any notice. I don't like that man's attitude."

"Me neither," I replied. "Thanks for telling me. It could be very important."

We climbed the stairs to the roof. Outside, the wind was bitterly cold. A woman was sitting on a low wall a few yards away from José. Detective Valdez from the negotiation team. José was sitting on the wall, wrapped up in a blanket from the operating room, with one leg hanging over the edge.

Stella and I cautiously made our way along the roof. I don't like heights, especially when the only protection from a fatal drop is a knee-high wall. We sat down beside her.

"Mr. Marley and Ms. Delgado?" she said in a whisper, with her face turned away from José. "I'm very relieved to see you here. The more people there are around that José knows and trusts, the more likely we are to talk him off the roof. Just keep your distance from him until he's ready to speak to you."

"José knows us as Nat and Stella. Are there any other officers up here?" I asked.

"No. I tried to get more in position, but José noticed them and started to panic. So I insisted on just one officer, and here I am," Valdez explained.

In situations like this, you never know whether a suicide threat is a desperate call for help, or if it's the real thing. It's a situation where nobody can take chances. The consequences could be disastrous. Detective Valdez continued with the routine that has saved countless lives in this city. The technique was to establish a relationship and gain trust.

"José, you know who I am now. I just want to talk," she said.

No response from José. He put the blanket over his head, so his face was hidden from view.

"I just want to know if you're listening. Raise a hand if you're listening to me," she asked.

José briefly raised his right hand. She continued in the same smooth, calm voice. "I've got some friends of yours here, Stella and Nat. They're worried about you. Do you want to speak to them?"

Again, no response.

Detective Valdez didn't give up. "José, just listen. You know these people. They're trying to help you."

Valdez tried patiently again and again. At last a reaction from José. He pulled the blanket off, swung his leg back from the edge, and stood up. All he was wearing underneath was a green surgical gown from the hospital operating room. The poor guy must have been freezing.

"What can you do to help me?" shouted José. "I got a murder charge hanging over me. What do I have to live for? . . . My head . . . I got this pain . . . It won't go away."

"Speak to him, Nat," whispered Valdez.

I stood up, trying not to look down at the drop below. "José, we've got new evidence. I can prove you didn't do it." That wasn't strictly true, but it might encourage him to come down from the roof.

"Then how come they've charged me with murder? How come?" protested José.

He threw the blanket over the edge. There was a sudden shock of panic below until it became obvious that it was the blanket rather than José that was falling. Then he sat on the wall, with his head down. Again, he swung one leg over the edge.

"What do you think?" I whispered to Valdez.

"Not good, but not a disaster. I'd like Stella to talk to him now," she said.

Stella's voice was cracking with emotion as she spoke. "José? Listen to me. I know you didn't do it. You're not a killer. Something happened to you after you left that bar and Nat's going to prove it. We'll get you off this murder charge, I promise."

Silence. Stella appealed to him again. José responded at last. "What do you have to promise with?" Now there was a change in his behavior. Words were coming slowly as if speech involved a major physical and mental effort. "I . . . don't . . . know . . . I'm . . . finished . . . My head . . ."

"What's happening?" asked Stella.

"I think he's going to jump," Valdez whispered. "But I don't want to frighten him with any sudden movements. Nat, get ready to grab him, but don't move until I say 'Now'."

José's body began to tremble violently. He began to rock his body from side to side.

"I'm . . . a . . . no . . . good . . . failure . . ." he muttered.

"Get ready, Nat," whispered Valdez. "Start moving in on him."

José continued muttering to himself, with his head lowered. Sometimes what he said made sense, sometimes it was just a confused string of words. I crept along the roof towards him.

"I'm . . . a . . . no . . . good . . . fail . . ."

As José's voice trailed off into silence, the sideways rocking motion continued. With each swing, the top part of his body hung for a moment over the vertical drop. Then the return swing.

Behind me, Valdez shouted urgently: "This is it. NOW!"

José had reached the furthest point of the swing. But this time he didn't return. He was slipping off the edge. I made a dive for his foot and just managed to grab it. José was now hanging upside down over the edge. I was also hanging over the edge, with only my knees pressed against the wall preventing me from following José. Stella and Valdez were already hanging on to me, but in that position, no one else could reach José from the roof. José was not light and I could feel my grip slipping. Valdez was screaming to the firefighters below: "Move it! Get that ladder up here before we have a fatality!"

I concentrated all my efforts on keeping my arm locked around his foot. José swung in space over the drop. I could feel my muscles aching and weakening. Then out of the corner of my eye, I noticed the ladder swinging round. At the top of the ladder, there was a firefighter, who took José's unconscious body into his powerful arms and swung him over his shoulder. As José was brought down to safety, a medical team on the ground was waiting to take him straight to the operating room. I pushed myself back from the edge and collapsed behind the safety of the wall.

I opened my eyes to see Stella kneeling beside me. "Nat, are you OK?" she asked. "You were wonderful!"

"Thanks. I'm alright. Just let me lie here. I don't want to

see that drop again just yet." I lay there for a while, thinking it was good to be alive, after all. I'd had quite enough excitement for one day.

"Nat, you're a hero," said Valdez.

"Well, if I'm a hero, so are you. You read all the signs that he was going to jump. Anyway, let's get down to the operating room and see what's happening."

We were informed that Dr. Ericson was already operating on José. The brain surgery was a delicate procedure which would take hours. There was also a high element of risk. José had already put himself in danger by escaping from the operating room. The added stress could only have done further damage. Stella decided to stay at the hospital and wait for news. As I left, she was calling her mother. A better option for me was home, food, beer, TV, and relaxation.

Chapter 6   *The Odessa Steps*

Monday morning, back at the office on East 43rd Street. I was going to be all alone. Stella had stayed overnight at Metropolitan Hospital. Her brother had come out of surgery but was still unconscious. It was still too early to tell whether the surgery had been a success.

I was now convinced that someone wanted a convenient fall guy to take the blame for Romanov's murder. Maybe José had simply been unfortunate enough to be in the wrong place at the wrong time. Just a harmless guy enjoying an evening out with his buddies. Now he was facing a murder charge. The problem was our total lack of evidence. The whole thing made me angry. But I couldn't allow that anger to affect my judgment.

Meanwhile, I'd done a little research on the cross that Edie Tilden had seen on the body on Jones Beach. It was definitely Russian – the design used in the Russian Orthodox Church. It was likely that the letters on the lifeboat were also Russian.

I now had photographs of José, Miguel, and Carlos. I'd phoned all the bars in the area and had finally discovered one run by a baseball enthusiast – the Odessa Steps. I decided it was time to take a trip to Brighton Beach and follow the movements of the three friends on Wednesday night. There was a small chance I'd pick up a few pieces of evidence.

As I was getting ready to leave, I had a surprise phone

call. Edie Tilden, the elderly woman I'd met at Jones Beach.

"Mr. Marley? Edie Tilden. Remember me?" she asked.

"It's kind of hard to forget you," I replied.

"You're not going to believe this, but I found two more bodies on the beach. Cold and stiff, they were!"

I gripped the phone tightly. "Now don't get over-excited. Just describe what you saw. Don't dramatize."

"Well, it was early this morning. I was out to see what the morning high tide had washed up along the shore. And then I found them. Two more young men. About five-hundred yards east from where the boat was wrecked," said Edie.

Edie went on to describe them. The two young men could have been anywhere in their twenties. Like the other two bodies, they were very thin. They were wearing cheap casual clothes: jeans, denim jackets, T-shirts, and running shoes. Clothes worn by young men everywhere; nothing specific to go on here.

"Did you notice any jewelry or identifying marks? Like scars?" I asked.

"No, nothing like that," she said.

"Thanks Edie. That's good work. You should have been a detective. Keep on with the beachcombing. Call me anytime you see something suspicious, will you?"

I was very curious. A murder in Coney Island, and now four bodies washed up on Jones Beach. Romanov was a respected member of the Russian community. And it looked like the four dead men found on Jones Beach were also Russian. Was there a connection?

I was wondering how those boys had died. Drowned

accidentally in a storm or what? I called the Coast Guard press officer, who had prepared a news release. He promised to email it to me immediately. As I put the phone down, the email came through.

<u>U.S. Coast Guard Group Moriches</u>
Press Release
Incident at Jones Beach, Long Island
The Coast Guard Service is currently investigating the wreck of a lifeboat discovered on Jones Beach and also the discovery of four bodies nearby. The victims are white, male, and aged between twenty and thirty.

The wreck is being investigated as suspicious for the following reasons:

No boats have been reported missing.

No person has been reported missing at sea.

The boat was not in seaworthy condition.

No registration details are available for the boat.

If you have any information that would be of assistance to the U.S. Coast Guard, please contact Commander J. Lockhart, U.S. Coast Guard Station Moriches, Long Island, New York.

I printed out the email and put it aside to read again later. It was time to go Brighton Beach and pay a visit to the bar where José had fallen asleep. I took an express Q train from the 42nd Street subway station. As the train made its way through the suburbs of Brooklyn, I glanced through the *Daily News*. Nothing more on the Romanov story.

I got out at the Brighton Beach subway station and started working my way along the avenue, inquiring at bars whether José and his buddies might have been drinking there. It was just before noon so the bars were still quiet. A couple of bartenders vaguely recognized the photographs but couldn't provide me with anything useful.

I finally arrived at the Odessa Steps. Inside, the walls were covered with baseball souvenirs: picture after picture of the famous Brooklyn Dodgers teams who dominated the American baseball scene in the 1940s and 50s. I ordered a beer and sat down to take in the atmosphere. The lunchtime crowd was arriving and the bar was becoming noisy with Russian conversation. At the next table, one of the staff had a collection of tools on the table and also, a beautiful antique baseball bat. He was preparing to put it on the wall.

"Excuse me," I said. "I'm interested in the bat. I bet it has a history. Something new for the baseball exhibition, huh?"

"This bat, mister, was used in the final game of the 1955 World Series," proudly replied the bartender, "when the Brooklyn Dodgers beat the New York Yankees. It's my boss's favorite piece. He paid a fortune for it."

"At today's prices, I'm sure he did," I said.

"Well, that was back in the 1980s, so it isn't a new piece. We've had it up here in the bar for years. You're not going to believe this, but Wednesday night last week, some joker pulled it off the wall."

"No kidding! Whoever it was would've been lucky to get out of here alive," I commented.

"I guess so," he said.

I showed him my investigator's license, and also the photos of José and his buddies.

"Did you happen to see these three guys in here on Wednesday?" I asked.

He immediately pointed at José's picture. "Hey, that's the guy who grabbed the bat!"

"What time was this?"

"Had to be nine o'clock. I remember because it was just before my break," the bartender replied.

"What happened to this guy after he tried to take the bat?"

So far the bartender had been talkative. Now he looked nervous and started to hesitate. "Er . . . I must have been on my break. Look, why don't you ask my colleague behind the bar. He'll remember."

The conversation with the other bartender followed the same pattern. His memory was perfectly clear up to the point when José took the bat. Mysteriously, they both suffered from total memory loss after that. Were they hiding something? Or were they scared of something? I was certain about one thing. If a stranger walked into this bar and attempted to steal one of their sports treasures, they'd be lucky to get away unharmed. Was it possible José received those throat and head injuries in the bar?

I didn't think I was going to find out anything more, but at least I had made some progress. José and his buddies had definitely been in the bar. I had a time, 9:00 PM, when José must have woken up, and in his confused state made a grab for the bat. But why wouldn't the bartenders reveal anything more? I stayed at the bar and ordered a roast beef sandwich and fries. While I was waiting for the food, I made a call to Stella at Metropolitan hospital. José was still in intensive care, slipping into a coma, a state of deep unconsciousness.

"Nat," said Stella. "My mom's going to take over for me at the hospital. I'll be going home soon to get some sleep. I'm just exhausted. But I'll be at the office first thing tomorrow."

"You know you don't have to if you want to keep your mom company," I said.

"Nat, I'm depending on you to clear José's name and prove his innocence. Let's get on with this investigation. I'm going to be right there with you."

Chapter 7 *Evidence*

Early Tuesday morning, on Main Street in Queens, the weather was just awful. It was pouring, with fat raindrops bouncing off the sidewalks. Car headlights were reflecting off the road surface, in places now inches deep in water. I splashed along the sidewalk. My hat and coat were soaking wet by the time I got to the subway station.

At East 43rd Street, it all seemed like a normal day. Stella was already at her desk going through the morning mail. She gave me her usual bright 'Hi, Nat.' But underneath that cheerful exterior, I knew she was deeply worried. As soon as I'd woken up, I'd phoned the hospital to get an update on José's condition. I was simply told: 'No change'.

The investigation into José's evening at Brighton Beach had made little progress. I'd also had a call from Lena Rosenthal. Oldenberg had given all the relevant police information to Lena, our lawyer. This included the autopsy report on Romanov. We had arranged a midmorning meeting at East 43rd Street.

Over breakfast, I did some thinking. I recalled the basic points of police procedure which I'd been taught years ago at the NYPD Academy. In every investigation, always establish M.O.M., which stands for 'Motive, Opportunity, and Means.' Motive – why did the suspect commit the crime? Opportunity – did the suspect have the chance to carry out the crime? Means – did the suspect have the weapon to carry out the crime? But when you applied this system to José nothing seemed to make sense. There's nothing out of the ordinary in a guy having too many drinks and waking up in a strange bar. But how and why could he suddenly come into the possession of a handgun, steal a car, and commit murder?

Later that morning, Lena was going through some of the details of Romanov's autopsy report with me.

"What worries me Nat, is timing," she began. "We know that José probably left the Odessa Steps at or around nine o'clock. According to this report, Romanov's time of death was somewhere between 8:45 and 9:45 the same evening. Now, for a drunk who'd just woken up, José would have to have been one fast mover."

"Agreed," I said.

"There's absolutely nothing to show how or where he came across Romanov," Lena continued. "Did he just walk out into the street, wave a car to stop, and then rob and brutally murder the driver? As I see it, there's no logic here. No supporting evidence apart from the forensics."

"Anything more in the reports?"

"Cause of death, a gunshot to the head at close range. Romanov was on the ground when he was killed. According to the report, there was bruising on his upper arms which could indicate the killer was standing on his arms when the fatal shot was fired."

Stella, who had been making some notes, suddenly interrupted.

"Ms. Rosenthal, I need to get something clear. The fingerprints that were found on the gun barrel. Right-hand or left-hand prints?"

"All right-hand prints, according to the report," Lena replied.

Stella said nothing but just looked down at the notepad.

"Stella, is José right-handed?" I asked.

Stella nodded. Another setback. If only José was left-handed. Another possible line of investigation closed.

Oldenberg had not followed official procedure after Dr. Ericson had reported the bruises on José's neck. With some minor blackmail, I could ask a favor. I thought I might have a talk with Oldenberg. I knew a subject that would hold his attention: baseball. His mind is an encyclopedia of baseball history.

"Oldenberg? It's Marley. Just called to tell you I've been admiring a bat used by the Brooklyn Dodgers in the final game of the 1955 World Series."

There was a low whistle of surprise from Oldenberg. I knew I had his full attention.

"It's a valuable piece of baseball history," I continued, "and you can see it for yourself at the Odessa Steps bar on Brighton Beach. They've got a whole museum of baseball stuff around the walls. But last Wednesday night, some guy pulled this bat off the wall."

"Hey, that would be terrible. That guy would be lucky to . . ."

"Get out of the place in one piece?" I suggested. "That's what people at the bar told me. And the guy is the accused, José De La Cruz. But he got out of the bar somehow. And then look what happened to him. Kind of strange, don't you think? Especially when the bar staff went suspiciously quiet when I asked what happened after José grabbed the bat."

"I don't know what to say, Marley. This information might have an effect on the case."

"Think about it. Now," I continued, "it's come to my attention that medical staff at Metropolitan reported bruising on De La Cruz's neck, which couldn't have been the result of the car crash. But you didn't order a medical examination of my client."

"How did you know about that?" demanded Oldenberg.

"Just doing my job," I replied calmly. "I have my contacts. I'm prepared to ignore this failure to follow official procedure if you do me a little favor. I need an official introduction from the NYPD to Lockhart, Commander of the Coast Guard Group in Moriches. That's the Long Island South section."

"What's this all about, Marley?"

"Let's just say another line of inquiry."

One o'clock. It had been a busy morning and I could hear a cold beer calling my name from McFadden's Bar. McFadden's Bar is just a block across town from the office, on Second Avenue, a favorite watering hole for New York journalists. I phoned the bar to check whether Ed Winchester was there. Ed's an old friend and a wonderful source of information. He'd been chief crime reporter for the *Daily News* for years, and still did some part-time work for the paper, though he was now officially retired.

No sooner had I entered the bar than I heard my name being called. A tall elderly guy with silver hair and a deeply-lined face was waving an empty glass at me.

"Nat, perfect timing!" Ed said.

"That must mean your glass needs refilling," I replied.

I took the beers over to an empty table and went though

all the recent events with Ed: Romanov's death, José's night out at Brighton Beach, the wrecked lifeboat, and the bodies on Jones Beach.

"You see, Ed, there seem to be Russian connections everywhere. I was just curious whether you'd heard anything about crime among the Russian community."

"Money laundering is the big one," he replied. "In international terms, the Russian ruble is seen as little more than toy money. So much of the real business of crime is done in hard currency, in U.S. dollars. A lot of illegal dollars from that black economy are probably coming in to the U.S.A. from Russia. The problem then is how to integrate that money into the legal economy here without attracting attention."

I'd heard about money laundering. Anybody running organized crime operations like drugs or illegal gambling receives huge amounts of cash. Thus the need for your friendly neighborhood money launderer to clean the dirty money by transferring it through a network of bank accounts until nobody can find where it came from. Once it reappears at the other end of the process, the money's clean and legal.

Ed called the crime desk to see if they knew of any money laundering activity in the Russian community. He listened carefully for a couple of minutes, then turned to me with a broad smile.

"There's a guy by the name of Victor Kamenev" he said. "It seems he was depositing regular amounts of cash, up to ten thousand dollars at a time, in a variety of banks around lower Manhattan. He's got a business – Kamenev Finance. Of course, there was the usual gossip at the crime desk as to whether he was laundering money for the Russian Mafia but no concrete evidence."

Ed had delivered the goods again, and cheap at the price of a beer. Another Russian name – but was there any possible connection between Romanov's death and the wreck on Jones Beach? I walked across town to First Avenue and wandered through the United Nations Plaza over to the East River. Walking time is thinking time so I just ignored the rain. I needed a way to gain access to the Russian community. Alexei Romanov's widow could be our entry key. But under the circumstances, we might have to be a little economical with the truth.

The initial approach to Mrs. Romanov would need tact and sensitivity – more Stella's specialty than mine. Back at the office, after describing the plan to Stella, she made that all-important call. Her telephone manner was, as always, perfect.

"Mrs. Romanov? I'm very sorry to disturb you at this extremely sad time. I'm Stella Delgado. My employer, Mr. Nat Marley, is investigating a matter which is of deep concern to the Russian community . . ."

After Stella had completed the call, we had an appointment for the following afternoon.

Chapter 8 *Mrs. Romanov*

It was one of those March mornings when the weather still hadn't made up its mind if it's the depth of winter or the beginning of spring. An icy wind was cutting across Manhattan. A few snowflakes were falling from the heavy, gray clouds. I'd arranged to meet Stella at Metropolitan Hospital, where she'd been at José's bedside with her mom. Stella was waiting outside the main entrance, shivering with cold.

"You'll catch your death of cold out here, Stella," I said.

"I prefer it out here. Right now I've had enough of hospitals. I've just been with José for an hour. There's no change. Still in a deep coma. Just the same as before. At least the police are being more relaxed about access now that he's unconscious."

"I'd like to see him anyway now that I'm here," I said.

We made our way up to José's room. As usual, the police guard was on duty outside the room. Through the window, I could see Stella's mom at the bedside, talking to the unconscious José.

"See that, Nat? Mom spends hour after hour chatting to him. She's convinced she's getting through to him. But I haven't noticed any kind of response."

"Let's hope it does some good," I said.

I didn't feel it was appropriate to enter the room. José was with his family. I knew that the unconscious brain can still be active and functioning. I just hoped he was receiving something, something that might get though whatever block was keeping him from regaining consciousness.

Yesterday, Oldenberg had emailed me a letter of introduction to a Commander Lockhart of the U.S. Coast Guard, who was based at the Moriches Coast Guard Station. I'd already made an appointment to talk to him about the Jones Beach wreck. The wrecked lifeboat was now being stored at Jones Beach Coast Guard Station, and I had arranged to meet Lockhart there. I was curious to examine it and prove any new Russian connections. As far as this investigation was concerned, it was all a very long shot. It could easily be a pointless visit. But I felt we should be doing something for José.

The subway was clear of the worst of the rush hour crowds. As the number four train sped downtown toward midtown Manhattan, I thought over what I knew about José's night out in Brighton Beach. If only he would regain consciousness, then he might recall something relevant.

From 51st Street, an E train took us west across town to Penn Station, where we took a Long Island Rail Road train to Freeport. A forty-minute journey, but quicker and cheaper than any cab. As the train made its way through the suburbs of Queens, I noticed Stella biting her lip. I know that little habit of hers; it means something is on her mind.

"Are you OK, Stella?" I asked.

"This past week, Nat, has been a total nightmare. I'm tense and anxious all the time. We seem to be getting nowhere fast. I know it's not your fault, you're doing everything you possibly can, but there are times when I feel like tearing my hair out and screaming."

"Don't give up hope, Stella," I said. "I won't let José down, believe me. I'm positive the evidence is out there. The pressure's getting me down too. If this was an ordinary, everyday investigation, I'd be able to walk away from it and put it right out of my mind. But it's there with me all the time. If I wake up in the middle of the night, I'm thinking about it. We'll crack this case somehow."

We took a cab from Freeport to the Jones Beach Coast Guard Station, where we were welcomed by the officer responsible for Long Island South, Commander Lockhart, a tall, fit-looking man in his fifties.

"Pleased to meet you, Mr. Marley," said Lockhart, shaking my hand with a firm grip. "Captain Oldenberg asked me to give you every possible assistance."

"Thanks," I said. "This is my assistant, Stella Delgado. We're working on a case that just might have a connection with the recent incident on Jones Beach. As you know, we'd like to see that wrecked lifeboat which was recovered," I replied.

Lockhart took us out to a workshop alongside the Coast Guard building. Inside was part of what had once been a well-built boat. The paint was peeling off it. Some clean fresh wood was visible where the boat had split in two. At the back of the boat were the faded letters. They did look like Russian letters.

Lockhart took a screwdriver from a workbench and pointed at a section of the boat.

"I'd like to demonstrate to you just how poor the condition of this boat is," he announced.

He drove the blade of the screwdriver into the wood. It went through with little effort. The wood was completely rotten.

Stella gasped. "Those poor guys!" she exclaimed. "They wouldn't have had a chance."

"This boat was no more than a floating grave," Lockhart continued. "It's completely falling apart."

"What about the four guys who were found on Jones Beach?" I asked.

"I have the full autopsy details in my office. Shall we go there and I'll show you?" he suggested.

Inside his office, Lockhart sorted through a pile of documents.

"Here we are. Cause of death: exposure and drowning. They must have floated for as long as they could. Maybe holding on to what was left of the boat. But the chance of survival in those temperatures would have been very slight," he said.

"Was there any form of identification on the bodies?" asked Stella.

"All that was found were some Russian labels on their clothes, and a Russian Orthodox cross. But otherwise, we've no identification. We're running a check with the Russian authorities, but these things take time."

"Off the record, what do you think really happened to these guys?" I asked.

"Our guess is an illegal immigration operation," Lockhart began. "They probably paid a huge amount of money for the privilege of being smuggled from Russia into the U.S.A. In cases like these, another bigger boat would be involved, probably a small fishing boat. They remain offshore, then transfer the immigrants into smaller boats."

"Are you talking about occasional incidents or regular shipments of immigrants?" I asked.

"We suspect regular traffic. We've had a number of reports of suspicious activity from routine Coast Guard patrols. The Coast Guard has carried out a number of search and seizure operations at sea, but our resources are limited. For every illegal immigrant we seize, there could be others slipping through the net. Of course, we question the ones we catch, but never learn anything really useful, like names of the people behind the operation."

"Thanks," I said. "This has been very useful. If I discover anything relevant, I'll let you know."

"Mr. Marley, whoever put any people into that boat might as well have been holding a gun to their heads," said Lockhart. "You realize there could still be more bodies? It could take time before they're all washed onto the beach."

From Jones Beach, we took a cab to Brighton Beach. The heavy clouds had begun to lift slightly and the occasional ray of sunshine was breaking through. Our next appointment – with Alexei Romanov's widow – had to be handled very delicately.

The Romanov house was situated in a wealthy neighborhood of Brighton Beach, off Shore Boulevard. Large houses with well-cared for gardens. None of the trees had been optimistic enough to think about bursting into leaf yet. The temperature couldn't have been much above freezing. The door was answered by a maid who took our names and left us waiting in the entrance hall.

Soon, she returned and led us into an elegantly

furnished dining room. Mrs. Romanov then entered – a tall gray-haired woman wearing a black dress with a simple gold pin fastened at her throat. In her face, you could see the grief that she must have been going through.

"Ms. Delgado and Mr. Marley. Welcome. Do sit down," she said.

"We realize that this is not an appropriate time to visit," began Stella. "We're aware of the good work your late husband did with newly arrived Russian immigrants, and we'd like to offer our deepest sympathies."

"Thank you. You're most kind," she said.

"Our visit concerns Russian immigrants who may have been attempting to enter the country illegally. You may have heard about the bodies found on Jones Beach?" asked Stella.

Mrs. Romanov nodded.

"They were probably young Russian men," Stella continued. "The boat they were sailing in was in a completely unseaworthy condition. Whoever was behind this immigrant smuggling operation had surely sent these boys to their deaths."

Mrs. Romanov frowned. I could see we had her attention. "But this is dreadful! Can I be of any assistance?" asked Mrs. Romanov. "Poor Alexei would have moved heaven and earth to bring the people responsible to justice."

I judged it was the right time to make my move.

"I realize that this is not a suitable time to ask this question, ma'am," I said. "We know your husband was active with the Immigrant Welfare Society. Could he possibly have made any enemies in the Russian community?

You see, there could be some connection between your husband's death and these poor boys found on Jones beach."

I really couldn't be absolutely sure of my facts here, but again, there was no harm in taking a chance if we were going to make any progress with José's case.

"The police have already asked me all about . . ." began Mrs. Romanov. She then paused and gave me a hard stare. "I don't think you're being completely truthful with me, Mr. Marley. What is the real reason for your visit?"

It was time to put all our cards on the table.

"Mrs. Romanov, I apologize. Yes, I have been less than honest. I am a private investigator representing my client, José De La Cruz, who, as you know, has been charged with the murder of your late husband. I do not believe that your husband was the victim of a simple street crime. I suspect your husband had discovered something that put his life in danger."

Mrs. Romanov's face grew pale. She sat silently and still as I continued.

"We also have to admit that our interest in this case is personal. Our client, José De La Cruz is Ms. Delgado's younger brother."

Stella turned to face Mrs. Romanov.

"Believe me, Mrs. Romanov, this is difficult for me too. As God is my witness, my brother is not a killer. Just a gentle, harmless, ordinary guy who must've been in the wrong place at the wrong time," said Stella.

I continued, "As far as the NYPD are concerned, they've found their killer, but I'm not convinced. I am asking for your help in finding your husband's real killer or killers. I can't be more honest that that."

Chapter 9   *Victor Kamenev*

Mrs. Romanov stood up and stared out the window for a moment before speaking again.

"Mr. Marley, Ms. Delgado," she said. "I believe you are sincere. You may count on my cooperation and support."

Stella looked at me and smiled.

Mrs. Romanov continued: "You appreciate this is a very difficult time for me. But I'll do my best. There's something quite weird about the events of last week. I've had this feeling that the police have not made every effort to investigate the case fully. Alexei was well respected for all his community work. He had a fine reputation. He made friends rather than enemies. I think of all the people he's helped to settle here and become good American citizens, and I'm not aware of anyone who could have anything against him."

"Did he ever mention any names? Any little remarks he made about people?" I asked. "Take your time."

"There is something. Last night, I was going through Alexei's wardrobe, seeing what I could give away to charity. In a jacket pocket, I found a piece of paper, rolled up into a ball. It was a short message in Russian with no date or address. It was a warning and just said: 'I am telling you this in the strictest confidence. Mossolov could be dangerous. You don't know what you're getting involved with.' It was signed 'Victor'."

"You still have the note?" I asked.

Mrs. Romanov opened a desk drawer and took out the

note.

"Does the name 'Victor' mean anything to you?" I asked.

"No," she answered.

"Well, it could be Victor Kamenev who runs a business by the name of Kamenev Finance," I said. "We'll have to check this out and get back to you. Have you informed the police about this?"

"No. There's just been so much on my mind . . ." she began.

"I'd advise you to let them have the note immediately, but with your permission, I'd rather you didn't tell the NYPD about Kamenev until I've checked him out first."

We left the house and made our way to the Brighton Beach subway and took an express Q train back to Manhattan. At last some pieces of the puzzle seemed to be falling into place, but we were still a long way from the solution. We had another Russian connection. I wanted to pay a surprise visit to Mr. Kamenev, but I needed support. We could be moving in deep, dangerous waters. I made a call on my cell phone to Joe Blaney, an ex-NYPD colleague of mine. Joe's also an ex-NYPD heavyweight boxing champion. He retired a few years ago but still looks impressively tough, tough enough to scare people into cooperating. That's one good reason why he accompanies me on any job where there's an element of risk.

"Joe, I have some work for you. Are you busy?" I asked.

"I got nothing on," said Joe.

"Meet me at McSorley's Ale House on East 7th Street at three o'clock, this afternoon. I'll give you all the details then."

Stella and I transferred to an uptown train at Broadway

and Lafayette, and got off at Astor Place in the middle of the East Village. Joe joined us in the bar just before three. I gave him a brief outline of the story so far before we left for Kamenev's office. On the stairs up to the office, old wallpaper was peeling off the walls. On the upstairs landing, flattened cigarette butts covered the floor. "Elegant, huh?" muttered Joe.

As we entered Kamenev's office, the contrast couldn't have been greater. Inside, all was clean, neat, and tastefully decorated. The floors were polished wood. Everywhere was the latest in office technology. In response to our request to speak to Kamenev, the receptionist said a little too automatically: "You don't have an appointment. Sorry, but Mr. Kamenev is busy with a client."

There was no sound of conversation coming from his office.

"Seems awfully quiet in there. Would you tell him Nat Marley wants to speak to him concerning Alexei Romanov."

She gave me a sour look and picked up the phone. She spoke briefly to him and then turned to me and said, "Seems that Mr. Kamenev's not so busy after all. You can go in."

The guy behind the desk had to be Kamenev, a big man with rosy cheeks, bushy moustache, and a full head of curly hair. You could see his reflection in the polished wood of the large desk. Around the room were various framed photographs of life in the old Russia from the nineteenth century.

"Mr. Kamenev? The name's Nat Marley, licensed private investigator. This is my assistant Stella Delgado and my colleague Joe Blaney. I'll come straight to the point. I'm investigating the recent murder of Alexei Romanov. I believe you may have information concerning who was responsible for the killing."

"I don't know anything. Who sent you here?" demanded Kamenev nervously.

Kamenev suddenly opened a desk drawer and produced an automatic pistol. He pointed it at me with a trembling hand. Joe was equally quick. His old police special was pointing straight at Kamenev, but his hand was rock steady.

"Mr. Kamenev," said Joe smoothly, "it's obvious you're no gunman. Let's use some common sense. I suggest you put that gun down."

Kamenev sighed and placed the gun on the desk. Joe moved to the desk, and emptied the bullets out of the weapon, then returned it to Kamenev.

"Is it true that you sent a warning note to Mr. Romanov?" I asked.

Kamenev eyed us suspiciously from behind his desk. "Before I say anything, I need to have a guarantee that you are genuine," he said.

"By all means. I suggest you call Alexei Romanov's widow," I replied and gave him the number.

A conversation in rapid Russian followed. After a while, he put the phone down and looked at us. "My apologies. You understand I have to be cautious."

I glanced around the room again. There were also photographs of the old Russian royal family. Nicholas, the last of the Czars with Czarina Alexandra.

"You obviously love your country. You must be a patriot.

Also, you must have been a friend of Alexei Romanov. Who were you trying to protect him from?"

Silence. After a long pause Kamenev spoke: "This is very difficult for me, Mr. Marley. It's really not wise to say anything more. If I were you I'd stay away from all this."

Kamenev looked uncomfortable. I wondered if he was too scared to talk, like the bartenders at the Odessa Steps? I tried a different approach. Kamenev's business could be benefiting from the money coming in from the illegal immigrant operation. I had no proof, but it was worth a try.

"I want to speak to you about some poor Russian boys found dead on Jones Beach. I've heard a rumor that someone was laundering the money these boys paid to get into the country, money that needed to be integrated into the legal economy. I understand that's your line of business."

Kamenev remained silent.

"Is money laundering part of your business?" I insisted.

Again Kamenev didn't say anything.

"Let's get one thing straight," I said. "I'm sure there's a whole lot of questions the IRS would love to ask about your accounts, but I'm not investigating your business. Let's get back to those poor young men who were washed up on Jones Beach. Whoever launders the money those boys paid to get into the country might as well have held a gun to their heads and pulled the trigger. Would it be you by any chance? You see, they died because they'd been put in a boat that was falling apart. The boat split in two in the storm and they drowned. In some way you might share some responsibility for the deaths of four good Russian boys."

I could see Kamenev's lips tightening. I knew what I said

had found its target. I was appealing to his sense of honor. I hoped and prayed there was some honor left in him.

"Four good Russian boys," I repeated. "All they wanted was to enter the land of opportunity and make a success of their lives. And now they're dead. Their families back in Russia won't know what's happened to them. Maybe they saved up for years to give their sons this chance. But you won't be out of pocket. The money will still be coming in."

"Honest to God," stammered Kamenev, "I don't ask questions! Their deaths couldn't be my fault."

"So you were just the honest money launderer, huh?" I asked. "No questions asked and nothing on your conscience?"

Kamenev remained silent. Sweat started to form on his forehead.

"I have this feeling there's a connection between Romanov's death and those boys found drowned on Jones Beach. You follow what I'm saying?" I went on.

He nodded, but his expression was blank.

"I think you can help," I continued. "Help us find the guys who sent those good Russians to their deaths. You're a patriot, and despite your line of business, I believe you're a man of honor. The most patriotic thing you could do is help us to find whoever is exploiting honest Russian people. We also want to find who really killed Alexei Romanov. That man did some fine work in the community, helping Russian folks to settle here."

He remained silent. I nodded to Stella. "Tell him," I said to her.

"Mr. Kamenev," Stella began, "our interest in this case is also personal. My brother, José De La Cruz has been wrongly accused of Alexei Romanov's murder. As far as the NYPD are concerned he's guilty. We believe he was set up as the fall guy, to take the blame. We need someone who knows the Russian community, someone who has the contacts and inside knowledge, to help bring the real killers to justice."

Kamenev took a deep breath and pushed his hands into his fists. "OK," said Kamenev, "I admit that in my work, I don't ask too many questions. Cash arrives from anonymous clients. I only know them by a number. But if innocent Russian boys have been killed and I've profited from it . . ."

I interrupted him. "You still haven't told me why you sent the warning note to Romanov. Who's Mossolov?"

"Mossolov runs some sort of operation in Brighton Beach and contacts me from time to time to expect a delivery of cash. We've never met, only exchanged coded emails and faxes. Monday last week, Mossolov emailed me and asked what I knew about Romanov. I asked why and the reply was that Romanov had been asking inconvenient questions. I didn't want to get involved, so I just played it safe and denied any knowledge of Romanov, except what's known publicly. I suspected that Mossolov was dangerous and so Romanov could be in danger."

"Thank you, Mr. Kamenev. Our problem is that we still have to prove who murdered Romanov," I said.

"Mr. Marley, I am a patriot, and I feel I owe a debt of honor towards my countrymen. How can I help?"

"I'm going to set up a meeting with Alexei Romanov's widow," I said. "I'd like you to be there. Expect a call from me tomorrow morning."

Chapter 10 *Witness*

It was now just over a week since Alexei Romanov had been found murdered. People's memories tend to fade once events become part of the distant past. We needed to find witnesses while their memories were still fresh. Maybe the presence of Kamenev would help the bartenders at the Odessa Steps to remember more about Wednesday night.

I left Stella to do some phoning to set up a meeting with Kamenev and Mrs. Romanov. I suggested somewhere like a good restaurant in the Brighton Beach area, but I left the choice up to her. I had received another Coast Guard press release. Another body washed up on Jones Beach. The details were similar to those of the other victims: a male, in his twenties. No form of identification on the body. No definite connection could be made with the previous fatalities on Jones Beach.

But if there was a connection, just how many people had been on board that lifeboat when it left the ship for the Long Island shore? With the information about deaths of innocent Russian boys, I didn't anticipate too much difficulty in gaining the cooperation of the citizens of Brighton Beach.

I had just finished reading the press release when the phone rang. I recognized the elegant English accent – Edie Tilden.

"Mr. Marley, I've seen a very suspicious incident, on Fire Island."

Had I been wise to encourage that eccentric old lady to play the investigator?

"Tell me all about it," I said.

"I spent yesterday beachcombing along the eastern tip of Fire Island. And I saw this man who didn't look like he really belonged on a beach," she said.

"What do you mean by 'didn't belong'?"

"He wasn't dressed properly. Too formal. He was wearing an overcoat over a gray suit. Shiny black shoes. He was looking out at the ocean through binoculars, but I don't think he was watching the wildlife."

"Could you describe him?" I asked.

"Well, he was tall, six feet plus, with a big build. But, you see, Mr. Marley, I saw all this from a distance. As soon as I got closer, he left."

Perhaps he was frightened by the sight of Edie Tilden. What she had witnessed could be relevant or could have been entirely innocent. Fire Island is the next narrow strip of land off the Long Island mainland, to the east of Jones Beach. Anyway, I stored away the information, thanked her, and returned to our immediate concerns.

Stella had made the necessary arrangements: a midday meeting at Café Paris in Brighton Beach. A table had been booked, and Kamenev was on his way to pick us up. It would be a pleasant change to travel to Brighton Beach by car instead of the subway.

Things with Kamenev were now more relaxed, so we were able to get to know one another a little better. Victor Kamenev's family, we learned, left Russia and settled in America many years ago. Like many in the Russian-American community, Russian was his first language, and he and his relatives had remained true to their cultural roots.

The car was now leaving Manhattan, crossing the Brooklyn Bridge. Below, the wind was whipping up the waters of the East River into white-tipped waves. Above us, on the footbridge, people were walking into Manhattan, well wrapped-up against the cold. Soon we were cruising along Flatbush Avenue, with the skyscrapers of Manhattan fading into the distance.

The conversation turned to recent events. "Mr. Marley," Kamenev started, "I've been thinking a lot about our conversation yesterday. I'll ask whatever questions you want me to. I can put pressure on people and ask for favors. There are people around Brighton Beach who owe me money. The prospect of negotiating a debt should encourage someone to talk."

The car was now rolling through the suburbs of Brooklyn. The rest of the journey passed sociably. On arriving at the Café Paris, we met Mrs. Romanov, who was waiting in the reception area. We were taken over to our table where I made the introductions.

"Mrs. Romanov. You've already met Stella and this is Mr. Victor Kamenev. Mr. Kamenev is as anxious as you are to get justice for your husband. Mr. Kamenev sent the warning note to your late husband."

Not surprisingly, Mrs. Romanov looked extremely tense. After ordering, Mrs. Romanov questioned Kamenev. A long conversation in Russian. To begin with, Mrs. Romanov's voice was sharp. I held my breath and crossed my fingers, but soon she sounded much friendlier. I breathed out. Then, they shook hands warmly. Mrs.

Romanov addressed everybody. "I'm sorry about that. I needed to be absolutely sure about Mr. Kamenev. Now, I feel I can trust him. This is a very difficult time for me. It's little more than a week since poor Alexei was so cruelly murdered. I want to thank you all very sincerely for coming here. Mr. Marley, I know you said your interest in this case was personal. Naturally, mine is too. I know you must have other work you should be doing, and this investigation must be a considerable expense."

"Well, not really, ma'am . . ." I began.

"Mr. Marley, you're a very poor liar. I'm hiring you to find my husband's murderer. Whatever the cost."

I could certainly use the money. I hadn't done any other work since I'd heard the news about José. And there was still the office rent, taxes, and salaries to pay.

"Thank you, ma'am, I accept. Stella will draw up a contract."

After a discussion over lunch, there seemed to be two clear avenues of investigation. One was the Odessa Steps. Having a member of the Russian community with us could help to make some progress there. The other avenue was Alexei Romanov's computer files, particularly those concerning the Immigrant Welfare Society. Computer skills were Stella's specialty, so she left with Mrs. Romanov to examine the computer, while I paid a visit to the bar with Kamenev.

When we arrived, the lunchtime crowd was building up. I took Victor over to the display of sports souvenirs. I showed him the baseball bat José had grabbed. The bat was now securely fixed to the wall with metal bands and strong screws. I gave Kamenev all the background information he might need about José's night out in Brighton Beach.

I recognized the bartender I'd spoken with on my previous visit. He was laughing and joking with the regular customers. His face dropped as soon as he saw me holding up José's picture.

"Remember me?" I asked. "I was asking you about this guy who'd been drinking here last Wednesday night. His name's José and he's in a lot of trouble. I got the impression you were suffering from a little memory loss. Or maybe you were just confused. I've brought a friend along to help you remember."

The bartender stood there silently. Sweat started to form on his forehead. He looked like a frightened animal, nervous and vulnerable.

"I didn't see nothing. I swear I didn't see nothing," he repeated.

Meanwhile, a smartly dressed guy, who I took to be the manager, joined the bartender.

"What's going on here?" he asked. "I'll have no harassment of my staff."

The moment he made eye contact with Kamenev, the manager froze and lowered his head. Victor spoke to him in Russian. It sounded like a heated argument at first, but tempers soon cooled. The manager waved to the bartender who poured drinks for Kamenev and myself.

"Mikhail, the bar manager, has just remembered how much in debt he is to me. I've offered to be flexible about the repayments, provided we get some information. Shall we move into your office, Mikhail?"

The bartender told us that José had woken up in the bar

alone. He was sleepy and confused. He stood up, reached out an arm, grabbed the baseball bat, fell over and just lay there. The regular customers at the bar were very offended. Who was this guy damaging the sacred bat? Before anyone could lay a hand on him, someone else had got involved and protected José from the furious regulars. This guy had taken pity on him and said he'd help get him home.

I was getting very interested indeed. There were a whole lot of questions I needed to ask via Kamenev's interpreting.

"The guy who helped José. Name?" I asked.

The bartender paused and looked fearfully toward his boss, who nodded his permission.

"He's called Nick Zernov. If you know what's good for you, you'll stay clear of him. He's a real bad guy."

That explained why he had the power to protect José from an angry crowd. Zernov had seen the opportunity to use José as the fall guy to make José appear guilty for a murder.

"Give me a full description of Zernov, will you," I asked.

"Tall, over six feet, and muscular. Black hair cut really short. Thick black eyebrows. His nose looks like someone broke it. Likes to wear expensive suits, shiny material."

I experienced that thrill you get when you realize some parts of the puzzle might at last be fitting together. I recalled Edie Tilden's description of the guy she'd seen on Fire Island. I had to remind myself not to get over-excited. We still had nothing concrete yet. I continued with the questioning.

"How drunk was José? Could he stand up?"

"He was a bit unsteady after Zernov picked him up, but

otherwise OK. He had a few more drinks and then Zernov took him outside. That's all I know," the bartender said.

"You know this guy José is facing a murder charge. They think he killed Alexei Romanov. José was just a harmless drunk. I don't believe he is the killer," I said.

The name Romanov meant something to the bartender. His face brightened. "Mr. Romanov helped me and my family. Such a good man."

I had a final question. "Would you be prepared to tell the police what you've just told us?"

Another discussion in Russian between Kamenev and the bartender. The bartender frowned and shook his head. Then he said something, almost in a whisper. Before I got the translation, I knew it meant 'No'. The bartender was clearly terrified.

Chapter 11 *Progress*

It was time to see how Stella had been doing at the Romanov house with the computer files. As Kamenev's car rolled along Shore Boulevard, I was thinking about the case. I told Kamenev my theory.

"Victor, I think we have enough new information to encourage the police to follow a new line of investigation. We now know that José left the bar with a guy who has local criminal connections. Zernov doesn't sound like the type of guy who'd rescue someone from a beating purely out of warm, sympathetic feelings toward his fellow men. So my theory is that Zernov saw an opportunity to use José as the fall guy."

"But what about all the evidence against your client? The forensics? And the murder weapon?" asked Kamenev.

"It'd be quite easy for Zernov to kill Romanov," I explained. "Then, for him to wipe the gun clean, grip José's hand around it, leaving his fingerprints on the gun. Even easier to do if José was already unconscious."

Back at the house, Stella had found something. A file protected by a password. Whatever she tried, family names or place names, she couldn't open the file. I glanced around the room. There were a number of photographs of old Russia. Opposite the desk was a picture of a wide avenue in a major city.

Mrs. Romanov noticed me studying the picture. "Poor Alexei loved that street scene," she said. "It's the Nevsky

Prospekt in old St. Petersburg. That's an idea! Why don't you try typing in 'Nevsky Prospekt'."

"Could you spell that out for me?" asked Stella.

Again, the computer denied us access. Stella keyed in the words individually, but still no success. Mrs. Romanov had another suggestion.

"That street is named after the Russian national hero, Alexander Nevsky. Try his name," suggested Mrs. Romanov.

Stella keyed in the words. This time the protected file opened. There were lists of dates going back over the past two years at regular intervals. Next to some of the dates were Russian names, sometimes with local addresses. By some of the names there was a capital 'M' with a question mark. The most recent date was last Friday. There were also a couple of future dates with an 'M?' next to them. The first of these was Saturday March 16th.

"What do you make of that?" asked Stella.

"Well, 'M' could stand for Mossolov," said Kamenev.

"OK. If we assume that Zernov works for Mossolov," I said, "and if we can find out what sort of operation Mossolov is running, then things should fall into place."

Mrs. Romanov had been examining the names and dates in the computer file. "Mr. Marley, I know some of these names. Some of them are people who Alexei helped through the Immigrant Welfare Society. This one here, Boris Tchernov, I know he entered the country illegally. Could Mossolov be smuggling in Russian immigrants? Could these be the dates when they were brought in?"

"It's possible, but we'd still need more proof," I answered. "I'd like to talk to Tchernov, but it would be helpful if you would accompany me, Mrs. Romanov, so there's someone he knows and trusts. But that will have to wait until tomorrow. It's time I had another talk with Captain Oldenberg. Stella, would you print me out a couple of hard copies of that file?"

We said our goodbyes to Mrs. Romanov and left with Kamenev in his car. Kamenev dropped us off at Police Plaza in Manhattan.

A sergeant led us to Oldenberg's office. Oldenberg was sitting with his feet up on the desk and didn't bother to remove them when we entered.

"Please don't stand up just for us, Oldenberg," I said.

"What made you think I would?" growled the captain. "I don't suppose you want some coffee."

"Thanks for the hospitality, but if it's NYPD coffee we'll do without it."

"Sensible decision. Now what can I do for you, Marley?" he asked, at last removing his feet from the desk.

There was the usual expression on the captain's face which seemed to say that life and work were an annoyance, and I wasn't making things any better. It was time to get him interested.

"The Odessa Steps, Brighton Beach," I began. "You remember I told you that José pulled that baseball bat off the wall and then got out of that bar unharmed? Well, the reason was that he had a protector."

"Go on, Marley. You're beginning to interest me," said Oldenberg.

"I also got a witness, but I doubt whether he'd give a statement to the police. A bartender saw José leave the bar with a big, smartly dressed guy. We have a name – Nick

Zernov. He's part of a local gang."

"How do you spell that?" asked the captain.

There was a rare burst of energy from Oldenberg as he swung around in his chair to the computer and typed in the name. A list of names came up on the screen, including a Nicholai Zernov.

"He's known as Nick, so this Nicholai could be the guy," I suggested.

Oldenberg opened the file. The photo matched the bartender's description. Zernov had a long criminal record. Like the bartender in the Odessa Steps had said, he was a guy to avoid. He'd been charged with murder but found not guilty and had served a four-year prison sentence for robbery.

"Oldenberg, I'm positive that's the guy who killed Romanov," I said. "Would you print me out a couple of copies of the picture?"

"So if he is, where's your proof?" demanded Oldenberg. "I don't have anything to charge him with."

"Well, let's provide you with more new evidence," I continued. "You already know about the warning note which Mrs. Romanov found in her husband's jacket. I've found the guy who wrote it – a Victor Kamenev, who owns Kamenev Finance. He has a lot of contacts in the Russian community. He discovered that Romanov had been doing some personal investigation into what could be an illegal immigrant-smuggling operation. But his questions had really bothered someone by the name of Mossolov. Kamenev knew Mossolov was angry, so he sent the warning note to Romanov."

"OK, let's check to see if there's anything on this

Mossolov," said Oldenberg. He typed in the name, but the screen remained blank. He paused and thought for a moment.

"If I'm going to charge Zernov, I need solid evidence. We have nothing on him except for the fact he left the Odessa Steps with De La Cruz. It'll be easier to find evidence against Zernov if he's under the impression that De La Cruz is charged with murder. You see where this is leading, Marley?"

"You mean the official NYPD line is that José is the killer, case closed. The unofficial line is that the investigation quietly continues," I suggested.

"You got it," said Oldenberg. "I'll have a police surveillance team watch Zernov's movements without being seen."

Suddenly Stella's cell phone rang. She rushed out into the hallway to answer it. There was a scream of joy followed by rapid Spanish conversation. She rushed back in to the room with tears in her eyes and grinning broadly.

"Nat! That was Mom. José's going to be all right. He regained consciousness this afternoon and he's been talking to her. The doctors think the operation was a success."

"That's great news, Stella. Now if you'll excuse us, Oldenberg, we need to get over to the hospital."

"OK, Marley," said Oldenberg. "I'll call the guard and tell him to expect you."

The rush hour traffic was crawling through Manhattan. To avoid the chaos on the streets, we took the subway uptown from City Hall to 103rd Street. From there it was only a few blocks walk to the hospital. Stella ran on ahead. I finally reached José's room, and through the window saw

Stella sitting beside the bed smiling at José. I knocked softly on the door. Stella came out into the hall.

"Nat," said Stella, "strict orders from the nurse. Don't get José over-excited. He can talk but it's all a big effort. He just needs plenty of rest. We've only been allowed ten minutes."

José recognized me as I walked in. "Nat, thanks for what you did on the roof. It's all a bit vague, but I'm told you saved my life."

"Don't worry," I replied. "Everything's OK now."

"What do you mean 'OK'?" he asked, trying to sit up in bed. "I'm facing a murder charge!"

"Come on, José. Just lie down and try to relax," said Stella. "You've got to rest." She smiled at him and gently stroked his hand.

As soon as José was calmer, I spoke to him again. "José, we've spent the last week investigating. We're turning up new evidence all the time. Just trust us. We're doing everything possible to clear your name. I want you to concentrate on recovering. Be a good patient."

"Nat, I can remember something," said José. "When I woke up in the bar, Miguel and Carlos weren't around. I stood up but lost my balance. I reached out and grabbed the first thing I saw to stop myself from falling. It came off in my hand. Then there I was, lying on the floor with all these angry guys looking at me. I can't remember what happened after that."

"Thanks, José," I said.

It was time to leave José to rest. I succeeded in persuading Stella to go home. Before going back to Queens, I thought I should stop by at East 43rd Street to check if there had been any messages. An email had arrived from Commander Lockhart of the U.S. Coast Guard. It read:

Dear Mr. Marley

Please contact me as soon as possible. We have some new evidence here that may be connected with the wrecked lifeboat and fatalities at Jones Beach. It's a Russian fishing boat, which was wrecked on Jones Beach last night. I'd like to show it to you.

Best wishes
Jim Lockhart
Commander, U.S. Coast Guard Group Moriches

I was very interested indeed. I called Lockhart immediately to confirm that I would be there in the morning. Enough investigating for one day. It was time to go home.

Chapter 12   *Wreck on Jones Beach*

After the recent storms, the weather was now calmer, with the prospect of spring in the air. I'd called Stella to tell her I was on my way to Jones Beach to inspect the fishing boat that Lockhart had told me about. Stella's instructions were for her to set up a meeting with Mrs. Romanov that afternoon. Lockhart had arranged to meet me at Babylon Station on the Long Island Rail Road, then to take me across the bay to the eastern end of Jones Beach to the site of the wreck.

It was an ancient-looking rusty boat. The force of the storm had driven it sideways onto the beach above the normal high-tide mark. It lay there on the sand and stones, leaning at a slight angle. Barriers had been set up around the boat. A Coast Guard officer stood by a ladder leading up to the deck. On board, Lockhart gave me the full story of what had happened. The previous day, in the early evening, the boat had been reported to the Coast Guard by a local fishing boat as a potential danger to shipping. Its engine had failed and it was drifting helplessly off Jones Beach. No emergency signals had been received. The crew of the local boat had tried to assist, but the offer of help was rejected. "Have a good look around," said Lockhart. "Tell me what you think."

I'm no sailor, but I wouldn't have felt confident out in the ocean in that boat. It had been some time since anybody had gone fishing in this floating wreck. I stuck my head into a cabin. On a table lay U.S. Navy charts for the south Long Island coast and New York Harbor.

"See those charts?" said Lockhart. "They're all up-to-date."

"What about the crew?" I asked.

"All four crew members were captured. The boat was kept under observation by a helicopter from the Cape Cod Air Station. As you know, there's easy road access to Jones Beach, so we picked them up as soon as the boat was wrecked. They were carrying Russian identification. They claim they don't understand a word of English, so we've arranged for an interpreter. Whether we get anything out of them is another matter. They've been taken to the Coast Guard First District headquarters."

Lockhart led me down below deck. There were a series of cabins fitted with beds with cheap nylon sleeping bags. There were signs of recent occupation. The air smelled of stale tobacco. On the floor lay Russian magazines, playing cards, smashed plates and cups, and the remains of a meal.

"According to my calculations, there's accommodation down here for fifteen people plus crew," said Lockhart. "This could be the boat that those poor Russian boys were in, but I can't prove anything."

"Five bodies so far. So if they had been shipped here on this boat there are potentially more fatalities?" I asked.

"Yes. It's unlikely there would have been any survivors from the lifeboat," said Lockhart.

I accompanied Lockhart up to the bridge. Inside, it was full of sophisticated equipment.

"The boat may look like a wreck, but they've installed the latest satellite navigation system," explained Lockhart.

"Look at this little device. It gives you your exact position wherever you are. My theory is the appearance of this boat is a deliberate disguise. From a distance, it looks like any other fishing boat. A perfect cover for smuggling in illegal immigrants. No ship's log, though, so we have no record of the boat's movements. If you come outside, there's one last thing to show you."

Lockhart took me outside. "Look," he said. "The lifeboat's missing. But I can't prove yet that the lifeboat wrecked on the beach came from this boat."

"So if you have this boat, does that mean it's the end of the smuggling operation?" I asked.

"We can't tell," he replied. "It wouldn't surprise me if they had several boats operating. Also, we have no idea how many smuggling operations are active at one time. We're going to double Coast Guard patrols off the south Long Island shore."

Back in Lockhart's car, I showed him the document from Romanov's computer file.

"Take a look at these dates," I said. "Are there any connections with incidents reported to the Coast Guard or that the Coast Guard has been involved with?"

After examining the list of dates carefully, Lockhart said: "Yes, there's a definite pattern here. Some of these dates match up. Where did you get this information?"

"From the computer files of an Alexei Romanov, who was found brutally murdered last week. I'm reasonably sure he was doing his own investigation of an immigrant smuggling operation. He must have asked too many awkward questions and paid the price."

Lockhart pointed to the final date on the list, which was

the next day, Saturday March 16th. "This could indicate another delivery of immigrants will arrive tomorrow."

I told Lockhart about what Edie Tilden had seen at the Fire Island – the big smartly dressed guy looking out to sea through binoculars. "Of course, it could be nothing," I said, "but I suspect he was checking out Fire Island as a possible landing point."

Lockhart unfolded a map of the Long Island beaches. "Let's suppose that a boat is going to be landed on Fire Island. There are lots of beaches but very limited road access across the bay. Any vehicle would have to return via Jones Beach from this point at the tip of Fire Island, and then there are only three points of access back to Long Island. They'd be caught like rats in a trap."

"Maybe, but you still wouldn't catch whoever's in charge of the whole operation," I commented.

Lockhart thought for a moment, then said, "I'll have to contact my superior officer and talk this over. I think the immediate plan of action should be a joint Coast Guard and NYPD operation."

Lockhart dropped me off at Babylon Station. I phoned ahead to Stella and arranged to meet her at Café Paris on Brighton Beach Avenue. She had already set up a meeting with Mrs. Romanov at her home. We had names and addresses of people from Alexei Romanov's computer file. To make any progress we would need Mrs. Romanov with us because of her status in the Russian community.

Stella was looking more bright and cheerful. The fact that José was at last on the road to recovery must have been a huge relief. Just as we were about to leave the restaurant to see Mrs. Romanov, there was a call from Kamenev. He'd been doing some research and had discovered a company called 'Mossolov Import and Export.' In my experience, a business which describes its function as 'import and export' could mean anything. It was a conveniently vague term that could apply to any number of activities. Was importing immigrants one of them?

"I'll tell you another thing," said Kamenev. "I phoned several times but just got an answering machine each time. When someone finally answered they just hung up without saying a word when I asked to speak to Mossolov."

"Good work, Victor. Do you have an address?" I asked.

The business was located on Brighton Beach Avenue. It would be worth checking out. A guy like Zernov wouldn't act on his own initiative. He wasn't paid to think. He would obey the boss's orders, and that boss could be the mysterious Mossolov. I passed on the information to Captain Oldenberg and also informed him about my meeting with Lockhart. More leads for the NYPD to follow up. Oldenberg promised to put an NYPD surveillance unit in place to watch the office.

At the Romanov house, I described the Russian fishing boat and its probable function to Mrs. Romanov. She listened carefully, obviously upset by what she heard. She turned away and held a handkerchief to her eyes for a moment. Then she turned back to me and told me what progress she had made.

Mrs. Romanov had already made contact with one of the people on the list, Boris Tchernov, a young man her husband had helped personally. She had made an appointment with Tchernov, who would come to her house.

Tchernov was in his late twenties. He was an immigrant who had been in the U.S.A. for almost twelve months. His English was good enough to communicate effectively without the need for an interpreter. He had met Alexei Romanov and was sincerely grateful for all the assistance he had received from the Immigrant Welfare Society.

"Mr. Tchernov, does the name 'Mossolov' mean anything to you?" I asked.

He shook his head. "I've never heard of it."

"What about 'Nick'? 'Nick Zernov'?" I asked.

I could see an anxious expression as I said the name. Tchernov knew all about him.

"I can tell you all about Zernov. Three years ago, I was living in Minsk, back in the old country. It was a hard life. There were ten of us living in a little apartment in one of the old Soviet buildings on the outskirts of the city. I'd always dreamed of a new life in the U.S.A. But it was difficult to emigrate legally. There's a limited number of visas available. I heard some gossip around that there were other means of entering the country. What you needed was three thousand U.S. dollars. A man called Nick visited regularly, made all the arrangements, and promised that jobs would be waiting for us."

Tchernov continued with more details of the operation: "Provided you had the money, no questions were asked. I finally met him. Exactly as I had imagined – well-dressed, successful. He told me stories about the U.S.A., the land of opportunity where any man could realize his ambition – as long as you had the dollars. I worked every hour I could, I borrowed, and, I'm ashamed to say, I stole. I didn't care how I got that cash."

"There was no question of flying us in. We were taken to the Baltic Coast, near St. Petersburg, to an isolated fishing port. I couldn't believe the boat they put us in. The conditions were awful – disgusting food, cold damp cabins, even rats. There must have been twenty of us on board. Crossing the Atlantic, one of the guys became seriously sick. He had terrible stomach pains. We begged the captain to radio for help, but he refused. The guy died after four days. They wrapped him up in an old sheet, tied a lump of concrete to his feet, and dropped him overboard. I don't imagine his family ever got a refund from Nick."

"The Atlantic crossing took about ten days. Most of the time it was stormy, we were exhausted and seasick. Finally we were all put into a small lifeboat in the middle of the night and dropped off on a deserted beach. Nick was waiting there with a truck. We were ordered to get in and lie on the floor and were taken to an empty factory building. I remember there was some sort of railroad track on the floor. We waited there and eventually we were taken in small groups to various addresses in the Brighton Beach and Coney Island area."

"Once we'd arrived, we learned the true reality of our situation. We were in the U.S.A. without entry visas and had none of the standard documentation. In effect, we were non-persons and totally in Nick's power. If I was discovered by the authorities, I could be sent straight back to Belarus. He could exploit us any way he liked. We were given really miserable jobs in kitchens or workshops, working twelve hours a day or more for very little money – and me with a good education. My life was being dominated by him. I escaped but found myself living on the streets."

"I was confused and didn't know how I would cope. Then, I contacted the Immigrant Welfare Society. Mr. Romanov was very kind to me and gave me money for food and rent. Such a good man. He was helping me with my application for a Green Card so I could become a legal resident. I was so shocked when I heard that he'd been murdered. Who could have done such a thing?"

Tchernov had come to the end of his story. I took out Zernov's photograph which we had received from Oldenberg.

"This picture was taken some time ago. Does this guy look anything like Nick?" I asked.

Boris examined the picture closely and handed it back.

"He's put on weight and lost some hair, but that's him."

Chapter 13   *A message from Mossolov*

It was almost six o'clock by the time we got back to East 43rd Street. The light on the answering machine was flashing. Stella pressed the playback button. A brief but threatening anonymous message:

"If you know what's good for your health, keep out of our business."

Someone was trying to warn us off and was prepared to use violence. But I wasn't intending to lose any sleep over it. We had done enough for one day and I told Stella to go home. I stayed on at the office for a while, sorting through some old case papers and filing them away. The phone rang. I grabbed it and said: "Marley speaking." But there was just silence. Exactly the same thing happened twice again, at fifteen-minute intervals. Whoever was at the other end wasn't talkative. I was starting to get suspicious. We have one of those phones that displays the caller's number. I tried calling the number, but there was no answer. Maybe someone was keeping track of where I was.

I put a call through to the Coast Guard to see if Lockhart had anything to report from their patrols off southern Long Island. Nothing as yet. It had been a long day, and the ideal way to finish it off was an appointment with a cold beer at McFadden's Bar.

Outside, East 43rd Street was practically deserted. Was it my imagination or was there someone watching me in the shadows of a service entrance across the street? I went over to investigate. Nobody there. Either my eyes were playing tricks on me or I was turning into a nervous wreck. Definitely time for that beer. I would feel more comfortable where there was noise, bright lights and company.

I ordered a large beer and stayed by the bar for a while, chatting with some of the regular guys from the *Daily News*. The tiredness was beginning to hit me. Time to go home. But I'd forgotten something. I patted my pockets and realized I'd left the keys to my apartment in the office.

Returning along East 43rd Street, I suddenly became aware of a large black limo following me very slowly. I turned around and started walking rapidly in the other direction. As I was passing the car, it stopped and a door suddenly swung open, blocking my path. I stepped aside to avoid the door, but a large, heavily built guy was already out of the car, standing directly in front of me. I immediately recognized the bushy eyebrows and broken nose: Nick Zernov. He was easily six inches taller than me. The street was completely deserted. If I tried to run, I knew Zernov, being younger and in better shape, would easily catch me. The only sensible thing to do was to talk.

"Good evening. Lost your way or something?" I asked.

Zernov's response was to lift me up effortlessly by my coat. His forehead was now level with my nose. That's what I call a serious invasion of personal space. I didn't like the idea of my nose being broken either.

"Marley, I have a message from Mossolov," said Zernov. "Stop asking questions. Don't stick your big nose in our business! Mossolov knows you've been watching us and wants you to call your people off. Otherwise, I'll have to break your legs. Is that clear, Marley?"

"Couldn't be clearer," I replied. "Message received and understood."

Zernov got back inside the car which sped off towards Park Avenue.

I'd learned two things from the meeting. First, that Zernov was definitely working for Mossolov. Second, Mossolov thought *I* had been watching them. They hadn't connected the surveillance operation with the NYPD. This was a possible advantage. If they didn't think that the police were involved, they might still go ahead with another immigrant smuggling operation. I'd have to contact Oldenberg to tell him to make the police operation less obvious. Then they'd assume they'd scared me off.

I went back to the office and called Captain Oldenberg. Fortunately he was still at his desk. I explained what had just happened.

"Do you have anything new on Zernov?" I asked.

"We have some good photos," Oldenberg said. "Zernov was twice seen entering the Mossolov Import Export office on Brighton Beach Avenue. But we haven't had a sighting of the boss of the organization. Zernov's been seen with two men and a woman on a couple of occasions. I'll email some pictures through to you."

One more call before I could go home. This time to Joe Blaney.

"Joe, I've had a serious threat made against me. I need protection. You'll need to be armed. And another thing, will you rent a car? Anything that's powerful but looks anonymous. Could you start this evening?"

"Sure, boss. I'm not doing anything else at the moment," Joe replied.

"OK, then. Pack a suitcase and come to my apartment at 9:00 PM," I said.

On the subway home, I immediately fell fast asleep but knew, as always, I'd wake up just before the train arrived at Main Street, Queens. It's a technique I've developed over long years of commuting. On Main Street, I bought a bottle of chilled white wine at the local liquor store and got myself a Korean take-out meal. It was my intention finally to have the quiet evening I'd promised myself.

When Joe arrived I knew I would sleep more soundly. It's reassuring to have an ex-NYPD heavyweight boxing champion sharing the apartment. Since I left the NYPD, I've never carried a gun. Normally, my philosophy is that if a job involves using a gun, it's a job not worth taking. That's on account of the potential health risks. I knew if Joe had to use a gun, he'd be more accurate than I could ever hope to be.

There would be no weekend break. I wanted to bring this case to a close.

Chapter 14　*Memories*

Saturday morning, the weather forecast promised clear, mild weather over the weekend. Perfect conditions for landing immigrants along the Long Island shore? Joe and I got an early start and had arrived at East 43rd Street by 8:00 AM. The light on the answering machine was flashing, a message from Mrs. Romanov asking me to call her urgently.

"Mrs. Romanov? Marley here."

"I'm so glad you've called. I've had some dreadful news." said Mrs. Romanov. "You remember the bartender at the Odessa Steps who witnessed Zernov leaving with De La Cruz? He's been badly beaten up. And not only him. The manager of the bar was also attacked."

"I'm terribly sorry to hear that. This is probably Zernov's work. He's making sure they stay silent," I said.

"Well, he's succeeded. They're absolutely terrified. I heard about this through contacts at the Immigrant Welfare Society. It was a brutal attack. That man Zernov must not get away with it."

I was just thinking about contacting Oldenberg and Lockhart when the phone rang. It was Stella, calling from Metropolitan Hospital.

"Nat, thank God I've caught you. I've been trying your apartment. It's José. His memory's returning, and he wants to speak to you. Can you get over to the hospital now?"

"I'm on my way," I replied.

José was looking much brighter. His head was heavily bandaged, but he was sitting up in bed. "Nat, it's all coming back," said José, "what happened on that night out. I can remember things now – places, people, faces."

Piece by piece, José put the story together. Everything matched what I already knew until he reached the point where he'd made a grab for the baseball bat.

"OK, now José, take it slowly from this point," I said. "Tell me everything you saw or heard."

"I looked up and saw this crowd standing over me. Wow! They were mad as hell at me. I couldn't understand what I'd done. Then I realized it was something to do with the bat. I heard someone shouting 'What the hell are you doing?' I was lying there, scared, surrounded by a bunch of real angry guys. Then someone pushed through the crowd and said: 'Don't touch him. He's mine. I'll take care of him'."

"What did he look like?" I asked.

"A big, tough guy, as tall as Joe here," said José. "He was wearing a shiny suit. Expensive-looking. He didn't look pretty. He had a face like a boxer who's lost too many fights."

"Sounds exactly like our friend Zernov. Go on, José."

"He picked me up off the floor. This guy's name, you said it was Zernov? Well he was holding my arm behind my back with a tight grip. Then he spoke again to the crowd, and repeated: 'I'll take care of him. Got any objections?'"

"Then he bought you a drink?" I asked.

"Yeah. He gave me drink after drink. I felt like I was

going to be sick but I was too scared to refuse. He started asking me all these questions. He wanted to know where I was from and what I was doing in Brighton Beach. Then he said he'd give me a lift home and took me outside. I tried to escape, but he was too quick for me. My arm was pushed up so far behind my back that I thought it'd break. He took me down a side street, pushed me up against a wall, and said, 'You're coming with me.' He grabbed me by the neck until I couldn't breathe. And that's the point, Nat, where everything goes blank. The next thing I knew I was here in a hospital bed."

"Thanks, José. You'll need to make a full statement to the police. Do you feel well enough to do that?"

"No problem," replied José. "But I want to get out of here. It's been nearly two weeks."

"It's not going to be long now," I said. "But you have to stay here under police guard, so Zernov and company think they've gotten away with it. Just hang on. The police are going to spread some misinformation. So whatever you hear on the news, or read in the papers, ignore it. It'll just encourage Zernov and Mossolov to remain under the impression that the police think you're guilty."

Back at East 43rd Street, there was a message from Captain Oldenberg. A joint meeting between the NYPD and the Coast Guard had been arranged for two o'clock at police headquarters. Oldenberg had invited me to attend. I put a call through to him.

"What do you want, Marley?" growled the captain.

"You sound full of the joys of spring, Oldenberg," I said. "Couple of things you could do for me. First, send an officer to Metropolitan Hospital to take a full statement from De La Cruz. His memory's returning, and it includes a positive I.D. of a guy matching Zernov's description."

"Sure," said Oldenberg. "Anything else?"

"I'd like you to spread a rumor, in advance of this afternoon's meeting. Could you arrange to issue a statement to the press to the effect that De La Cruz will be released from the hospital today and taken to Rikers Island prison before his trial for the murder of Romanov. I want this distributed to all the local radio and TV stations, and I also want it in the Sunday newspapers. My theory is, the more misinformation you create, the more likely Mossolov is to make a move."

"You got it, Marley. I'll have the press office get on to it immediately. And those pictures of Zernov that I promised you. I'll email them now."

Oldenberg was true to his word. Within minutes the photos arrived. The picture quality wasn't great but there was enough detail there to make out Zernov, looking huge and ugly, as normal. "What do you think of these?" I asked Joe.

"Well, he's been getting around a lot lately and meeting a lot of people." He pointed to one of the pictures showing Zernov opening the limo door for a big man in an expensive suit and dark glasses. "Is that Mossolov do you think?"

"Could be," I answered.

In the next photo, the same man was standing next to a woman with long dark hair. "And who's the woman? Another colleague? Mossolov's wife?" I said.

I looked out the window. As promised on the early weather forecast, it was clear and calm. These conditions would be exactly what Mossolov needed to bring in the next boatload.

A call came through from Lockhart to confirm that he would be present at the afternoon meeting. He also brought me up-to-date on the latest developments from the Coast Guard end.

"One of the captured crew members decided to talk. I'll email a copy of the statement in advance of the meeting. It makes for interesting reading. There's strong evidence that the casualties on Jones Beach and the wreck of the fishing boat are connected."

As soon as the email was printed out, I glanced quickly through it until I came to the relevant section. Then I read slowly and carefully.

We were carrying ten Russian immigrants. The captain stopped about a kilometer off shore, and the men were loaded onto the lifeboat. We had complained to the captain about the condition of the lifeboat. The captain ignored the complaints.

A signal was received from the shore. Then the lifeboat set off towards the light. When it had covered about half the distance, the weather changed rapidly. A storm blew up. We could see that the boat was in trouble. They couldn't seem to control it. I guess the motor had broken down. Then we lost sight of it. I begged the captain to move in and pick up any survivors. Eventually he agreed, but by the time we reached the area, there was nothing to be seen. We were now in danger of being driven onto the shore ourselves, so we had to leave and head out to sea.

It was then that we started to have engine trouble. The

captain tried to steer away from the Long Island shore, but the engine was gradually losing power. Day after day, we tried to fix the engine, but nothing worked. Eventually, a combination of wind and currents started to push the ship back towards the coast. When the next storm blew up, the motor finally failed completely. We were helpless. Also, we didn't have a life-boat to escape in. Our boat was finally wrecked on Jones Beach, and the crew members were arrested by the Coast Guard.

I continued reading through to the end. No mention of any names of the people who could be behind the operation. If there was no connection here to Zernov and Mossolov, maybe they would still go ahead with an attempt to land illegal immigrants.

Chapter 15 *Closing the net*

As Joe drove me downtown on Second Avenue to police headquarters, I turned on the car radio and checked the local radio stations to see if I could find any news. I caught a bulletin on WNYC. Oldenberg's press office had achieved everything I could have hoped for. José was named as having been arrested and charged with the murder of Alexei Romanov.

Perfect. The publicity would, hopefully, deceive Zernov and Mossolov. As long as they were acting under a false sense of security, they might proceed with bringing in the next shipment of immigrants.

At police headquarters, Oldenberg and Lockhart were reviewing the case.

After a while, I spoke up: "Let's assume that Romanov was murdered on Mossolov's orders because he knew too much about their operation. At least some of the dates we found on Romanov's computer are the same dates when the smuggling operations took place. We have a future date on that list. Now assuming the shipment will be landed on Fire Island, then it should be a simple surveillance operation to follow any vehicle to its destination. That's where we should strike. I doubt whether Mossolov is going to run the risk of hanging around exposed beaches."

"All seems logical enough to me," said Lockhart.

"Now we already know that Mossolov Import and Export is located on Brighton Beach Avenue. I don't believe the immigrants will be taken there. It'd be too obvious. I know from Boris Tchernov's statements that the immigrants were taken to some sort of factory building in the Coney Island area. I would suggest that any vehicle they use to move the people is followed at a very safe distance, maybe by NYPD helicopter. Then have police units standing by in the Coney Island and Brighton Beach area."

Oldenberg and Lockhart then proceeded to organize the combined NYPD/Coast Guard operation. The plan was to have a Coast Guard patrol boat out at sea observing any movements there. Also, a Coast Guard helicopter from Air Station Cape Cod would be on patrol and Coast Guard officers would be posted along Fire Island at regular intervals. The police part of the operation was to observe all road exit points from the beaches to the mainland and report to the NYPD helicopter, which would then follow the suspicious vehicle. Four unmarked NYPD cars would be placed along the length of Neptune Avenue, ready to pursue the vehicle to its final destination.

I had a special request to make. "Oldenberg, I'm not in the habit of asking favors from you, but I want to be in on this operation with my colleague Joe Blaney. You realize that I've provided the NYPD with most of the information in this case so far?"

"Yes," replied Oldenberg.

"And you know my personal interest in this case. I want to prove, without any doubt, that De La Cruz is innocent. And also, I want to find out who killed Romanov. I need a confession. That's why we have to be there at the finish."

"You're both ex-NYPD, so you're well aware of the

risks," said Oldenberg bluntly. "You have my permission, but don't even think about playing the hero, Marley. Understood? We'll have all units in position by dusk, and I'll keep in regular contact with you by cell phone."

Joe and I had little else to do until nightfall. Before leaving for Coney Island, I put a call through to Stella to give her an update.

"Nat, those news bulletins!" exclaimed Stella. "They're just awful! What a relief they're not true! I've had calls from just about every relative in the family about the news. I just had to tell them not to worry."

"Well, if those bulletins have fooled all your family, let's hope they have the same effect on Zernov and Mossolov," I remarked.

Another call to Mrs. Romanov to inform her of the real purpose of the bulletins and to reassure her that we were making definite progress.

"I'm reasonably optimistic that your husband's killer will be behind bars by tomorrow," I said.

"Take care, Mr. Marley and God be with you," she replied.

We headed off in the rental car towards the Brooklyn Bridge. Through the steel network I could see that the waters of the East River were smooth and calm, with the late afternoon sunshine reflecting off the surface. We passed rapidly through the suburbs of Brooklyn on Ocean Parkway, which eventually brought us onto Surf Avenue, parallel to the oceanfront.

We had some time to kill, so I asked Joe to continue west along Surf Avenue. The amusement parks, dominated by the huge roller coaster rides soon came into view. One of those rides which had terrified and delighted me as a child was still operating – the Cyclone. I still remember the way the train of little cars would climb up the track to the highest point, then dive and shake down what felt like a series of near-vertical drops.

There was another roller coaster ride standing behind locked gates. I examined the curves and slopes. Now I recognized it as the old Thunderbolt, another childhood favorite. Sadly, it was now in a state of total disrepair with peeling paintwork, rust, and fire damage.

The sun was now sinking low and the western sky was glowing with shades of orange and pink. It was going to be a long night.

It was completely dark when I received the first call from Oldenberg. The Coast Guard had been following the movements of ships off the Long Island coast all day. As the light faded, a fishing boat had turned towards the shore and was now heading in the direction of Fire Island.

"It looks like it's all happening, Joe," I said. "Time to get in position."

Chapter 16 *Face to face*

Time seemed to drag as Joe and I sat waiting in the car, in a parking lot off Neptune Avenue. Joe had brought a police radio with him so we could listen in on the action. I didn't want to feel we were missing any of the excitement. Soon after ten o'clock, we received a report of the first definite sighting from Oldenberg. Coast Guard observers had watched a small boat land a party of ten men and four packages at the eastern end of Fire Island. A white Ford truck had arrived, driven by a tall, heavily built guy who matched Zernov's description. The truck had picked up the men and the packages and had been spotted leaving Fire Island. Later, Oldenberg informed us that the truck was now on Long Island Highway 27, heading toward Freeport. The NYPD helicopter was following its movements at a safe distance.

It was around eleven o'clock when we heard that the truck was approaching the Coney Island area. The helicopter pilot was having trouble following the vehicle. An ocean storm was brewing, and a lot of fog was rolling in. Not ideal conditions for surveillance from the air.

The pilot now reported that the truck was on the eastern side of JFK airport, on the Belt Parkway, which circles the coast around Jamaica Bay. Frequent banks of fog continued to make observation from the air a problem. Then we heard a panicky note in the pilot's voice. "Captain Oldenberg, we're losing him . . . No, there he is again . . .

This is getting difficult. There's more fog ahead. Lost him. No, we've got him again. Captain, we may not be able to keep the suspect under surveillance. The truck's heading east on the Belt Parkway now. I suggest you move all units now to the Belt Parkway exits for Coney Island."

Finally we heard the pilot admit defeat. "Captain Oldenberg, we've lost him."

There was radio silence for a time. Then a sighting of the truck leaving the Belt Parkway at exit seven and heading towards Ocean Parkway.

A call from Oldenberg: "Marley, the truck's in Coney Island, on Ocean Parkway. I have one unit already following, and I'm ordering all units in. I'll keep you posted."

We continued listening in on the police radio. At first everything went smoothly until the intersection at Brighton Beach Parkway. An officer was speaking to Oldenberg: "Captain, we have the suspect in sight. We're about fifty yards behind. Red light, coming to a stop. Hey! He's run right through the red light."

"Try and follow," ordered Oldenberg.

Suddenly, over the radio, we heard the scream of tires followed by two impacts of steel against steel. Then silence.

"Captain Oldenberg," said the officer. "We just ran into the side of a cab, and our other car is buried in the back of our car. Nobody hurt, just shaken up. Sorry, but both cars are out of action."

"Where's the third car?" shouted Oldenberg. "Get after the suspect!"

"Sorry Captain. The traffic's now at a standstill at the intersection. Nothing's moving. The third car can't get through. We've lost him."

"Hell!" swore Oldenberg.

A moment later, Oldenberg called me on the cell phone. "Marley. I hate to admit this . . ."

"But you've lost the suspect," I finished for him. "We know, Oldenberg. We've been listening in on the police radio. Joe and I are going to cruise around the neighborhood, just in case we spot something. I suggest you do the same."

I asked Joe to head towards Surf Avenue. Soon we were passing by the amusement parks, with the ghostly shapes of the big wheels and roller coasters appearing out of the fog.

As we made our way along the avenue, I started thinking about the surveillance photographs of Zernov. Suddenly, every piece in the puzzle joined together to give me a complete picture. That photograph of Zernov outside a set of gates. I thought back to our tour of the sights of Coney Island. The old Thunderbolt roller coaster. The gates with the peeling paint. Boris Tchernov's statement that they were taken to some sort of factory building with a railroad track on the floor. I knew then where they had to be.

"Joe, the old Thunderbolt roller coaster. And step on it."

The car sped towards West 16th Street, off Surf Avenue. As we approached the roller coaster, the ruined structure gradually came into focus through the fog. I told Joe to kill the headlights as we neared the gates. All was quiet and the street was deserted.

Signs reading 'Dangerous structure – No admittance' were attached to the fence surrounding the old ride. The gates were at least ten feet high but with Joe's help I climbed over. On the other side, there was a lock and key with a thick steel chain. I tried the key in the lock. It turned without any effort. This entrance was obviously used regularly. I opened the gates to let Joe through.

We looked around us. Now, there was sufficient moonlight to provide better visibility. About seventy-five yards away, I spotted a white Ford truck and a limo parked alongside a one-story building in the shadows of the roller coaster structure. No lights could be seen.

A door opened. A sudden flash of light from the interior of the building, then darkness.

"Get down!" I whispered to Joe. We dived for cover behind an ancient roller coaster car. I looked over the edge and watched. It was Zernov. He started to walk in the direction of the gates, shining a flashlight from side to side. We kept our heads low as the ray of light was directed towards us. Then he went back inside. My mouth was dry and my heart was beating like a drum.

"Joe, we need back-up. Zernov's in there, and presumably Mossolov. There could be more of the gang inside."

I called Oldenberg and gave him our location. "When you arrive, I want you to park so your car's blocking the gate, OK? Same for the other police car. Then we'll have the exit sealed. But hurry!"

Oldenberg made rapid time. Two minutes later we heard the deep hum of the engine. Oldenberg and his sergeant slipped inside the gates.

"Over here," I whispered to Oldenberg. "Where's the other car?" I demanded. Oldenberg spoke urgently into his cell phone. His officers had gone to the wrong roller coaster.

Oldenberg considered the situation for a moment, then announced: "We're going in. All the evidence should be there. Any delay could mean we lose the key players. You with me, Marley?"

"All the way, Oldenberg."

We hurried over to the door of the building. From inside, we could hear conversation in Russian, and laughter. Although there were only the four of us, we had the element of surprise.

Oldenberg, the sergeant, and Joe had their weapons ready. Oldenberg nodded to his sergeant, who kicked the door wide open. We rushed inside. The sergeant shouted: "Police! Don't move! Hands in the air!"

For a second, the scene before us seemed to be frozen in time. The building was lit by oil lamps. Ten young men were sitting on benches around a table, drinking coffee and eating sandwiches. Zernov, who was sitting at another table, stared at us in disbelief. The big man from the photographs was there sitting next to Zernov. The woman with long dark hair was standing behind them. On the floor was the railroad track which Tchernov had mentioned. In a corner lay an old roller coaster car, on its side. The place must have been the repair workshop.

The woman didn't seem to be alarmed at all. Zernov looked towards her, with a confused expression, as if expecting instructions. Then she turned towards Zernov and screamed: "Don't just stand there. Do something!"

He suddenly got up and reached for his gun, but before he could aim it, two shots rang out. He spun around with the impact of the bullets. Then he crashed to the floor, firing his gun wildly. A bullet passed through one of the oil lamps, smashing the glass. A cloud of gunsmoke hung in the air.

The place now seemed unnaturally quiet. For a second everyone stood motionless. Then we rushed forward. There were two bullet holes in Zernov's chest. Blood was dripping from his mouth and he was gasping for breath. He didn't look as if he had long to live. Meanwhile, the woman had thrown herself to the ground and had landed in a pool of rust-colored, oily water. As she raised herself, her face and hair and were dripping with the orange-black liquid.

I looked at the guy still sitting at the table. "Are you Mossolov?"

He stared at me, almost paralyzed with fear. "I'm just the driver," he stammered. "Don't shoot me."

The woman was now wiping the oil from her face. She looked down at her feet, not making eye contact with anybody.

Then, a slight movement from Zernov. With a painful effort, he slowly pointed a bloody finger towards the woman. Then the gasping stopped. His eyes open wide in a lifeless stare.

We looked at the woman in astonishment. Was she Mossolov? She remained standing there, looking down at the floor. The woman's handbag was lying on the table. I quickly found a driver's license: Katarina Mossolov. I showed the document to Oldenberg. "Let me introduce you to Mossolov," I said.

"Well, would you believe it!" exclaimed Oldenberg.

Everybody's attention was focused on Mossolov. But suddenly there was the sound of rapid footsteps. "Hey, where's the driver?" asked the sergeant urgently. From outside, we heard the sound of a motor. Then tires spinning and screaming as the limo raced to the gates.

"He won't get far," remarked Oldenberg.

Then came the crash of breaking wood and bending metal. Footsteps running down the street. A shout: "Police! Stop right there!" The other police car had finally arrived.

"They've got him," said Oldenberg. "From the sound of the crash, that's another NYPD car out of action. Still, cars are replaceable, good officers aren't."

I had one last favor to ask Oldenberg. "Before you charge Mossolov, I want a word with her. Just trust me, OK?"

She looked at me blankly. Oily liquid was still dripping from her hair.

"I don't enjoy being threatened," I said to her coldly. "The last time I met your man Zernov, he promised to break my legs if I didn't behave. Now look at him. The NYPD already has enough evidence against you to put you away for a very long time. The only choice you have is to cooperate. Unless you'd like my muscle man Joe to help persuade you."

I must have sounded convincing. I knew it was an empty threat, but she believed me. She looked around in alarm. Joe grinned unpleasantly at her to back up the message.

"So tell me. Did you have Romanov murdered?" I asked.

"All right. I admit it. I ordered Romanov's death," she said in a low, tired voice. "He knew too much and had been asking too many questions about my operation. Nick was carrying out my orders. But the fool made everything too complicated. I told him to make it look like a simple car-jacking. Nothing fancy. Then he found that stupid drunk in the Odessa Steps. I don't know who was more stupid, Nick or the drunk. Not that it matters any more."

I had the confession I wanted. Case closed. "Oldenberg, did you catch all that?" I asked.

"Everything, Marley. And I didn't hear you making any threats. May I congratulate you."

That was a compliment indeed, coming from the captain.

"Thanks. She's all yours now. Will you arrange the immediate release of De La Cruz? He'll need a statement to the effect that he was wrongfully arrested and charged, and of course an official apology from the NYPD. His lawyer will also be asking for financial compensation for wrongful arrest."

"You got it," replied Oldenberg.

My hands started to tremble violently. I knew that old familiar reaction to shock. I felt a wave of exhaustion going through my body. But there were still two more things I had to do; first a call to Mrs. Romanov.

"Mrs. Romanov? I know who murdered your husband. Nick Zernov acting under the orders of a Katarina Mossolov, the woman behind the immigrant smuggling. Zernov is now dead and Mossolov is under arrest. You'll get a full report on Monday."

"Thank God you're safe," said Mrs. Romanov. "I can't thank you enough."

And a call to Stella. "It's Nat. We have all the proof. José's going to be a free man. We've cleared his name."

"Oh, Nat, I'm so relieved. I don't know what to say. It's like huge weight's been lifted from me. I'll have to phone around to all the family right now."

"You do that, Stella. I'll see you on Monday."

I took one last look around the repair shop. The glow of the oil lamps, Zernov lifeless on the floor, dead eyes staring into empty space, Mossolov now in handcuffs, with an expression of complete disbelief. The illegal immigrants were still sitting at the table, looking around in shocked silence. What an introduction to the U.S.A., the land of opportunity! Time to get back to some of that predictable, routine work like divorce, bad debts, and missing persons. It was safe and dull, paid the bills, and didn't involve being shot at.

"Come on, Joe. That's quite enough excitement for one night. Let's go home."

Cambridge English Readers

Look out for these other titles in the series:

Level 5

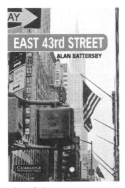

East 43rd Street
by Alan Battersby

New York, six days before Christmas. Nathan Marley is relaxing in McFadden's Bar. A woman walks in and out of the bar and Marley follows her. Christmas is about to become a lot more exciting for Marley.

Emergency Murder
by Janet McGiffin

When the wife of a surgeon dies suddenly in a hospital in Milwaukee, USA, Dr Maxine Cassidy suspects murder. When someone tries to kill her, she wonders which of her colleagues she can trust.

Level 6

A Tangled Web *by Alan Maley*

Dan Combes is a former MI6 agent. After being attacked, he realises his relationship with the British secret service has not finished. He believes the attack is linked to his work five years ago. But why do they want him dead now?

The Sugar Glider *by Rod Neilsen*

Pilot Don Radcliffe returns to Australia hoping to spend more time with his daughter, Judy. But a routine cargo flight turns into tragedy when the plane crashes, killing the co-pilot. Dan and Judy's chances of survival seem slim.

Level 6

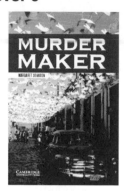

Murder Maker
by Margaret Johnson

After her boyfriend leaves her, Carla wants revenge. She meets three women who have also been abandoned by their partners. Carla decides to practise her revenge on these men and starts by buying a ticket to Cuba. . .

Deadly Harvest
by Carolyn Walker

Chief Inspector Jane Honeywell is a city detective in a sleepy country town. The peace and quiet is suddenly disturbed by a particularly horrible murder and Jane starts the dangerous pursuit of the killer, or killers.

Trumpet Voluntary
by Jeremy Harmer

A musician disappears leaving only a strange e-mail message behind her. Her husband, in a desperate search to find her, revisits their shared past. His journey of discovery takes us across the world to Rio and deep into the human heart.

Frozen Pizza *by Antoinette Moses*

These highly enjoyable stories offer eight slices of life in England today. Themes include inner-city problems, immigration, football hooliganism, food, student life, leisure activities, the media and the countryside.